THE LAST BENCH

Adhir Biswas was born in 1955 in the village of Magura, in the Jessore district of erstwhile East Pakistan. His family moved to Calcutta in 1967. He began writing in magazines in 1976 at a friend's prompting, and is the author of twenty-two volumes of fiction and non-fiction, including two sets of refugee memoirs, and two childhood memoirs. He was awarded the West Bengal Bangla Academy's Suprabha Majumdar Memorial Prize in 2014 for his refugee memoir, *Allahr Jomite Paa*, and the Vidyasagar Prize in 2017 for his four-volume collection of stories, novellas and novels for young readers, *Udojahaj*. Adhir Biswas established the publishing house Gangchil in 2005. He is currently the publications editor of the Dalit Sahitya Academy in West Bengal.

V. Ramaswamy is a translator of voices from the margins. Among the writers he has translated from West Bengal and Bangladesh are Subimal Misra, Manoranjan Byapari, Mashiul Alam, Shahidul Zahir, Swati Guha, Shahaduz Zaman and Ismail Darbesh. His translation of Adhir Biswas' refugee memoir, *Memories of Arrival: A Voice from the Margins*, was published in 2022. *The Last Bench* was selected for the inaugural PEN Presents award in 2022.

THE LAST BENCH

ADHIR BISWAS

TRANSLATED BY V. RAMASWAMY

ekadā

ekadā

First published in Bengali as three separate books, *Achhoot Baloker Classroom, Ei Dupur, Chup Dupur* and *Ei Amader Gram, Ei Amader Bari,* in 2019, 2022 and 2020 respectively by Gangchil

Published in English as *The Last Bench* in 2025 by Ekadā, an imprint of Westland Books, a division of Nasadiya Technologies Private Limited

No. 269/2B, First Floor, 'Irai Arul', Vimalraj Street, Nethaji Nagar, Alapakkam Main Road, Maduravoyal, Chennai 600095

Westland, the Westland logo, Ekadā and the Ekadā logo are the trademarks of Nasadiya Technologies Private Limited, or its affiliates.

ISBN: 9789360456818

10 9 8 7 6 5 4 3 2 1

Typeset by Jojy Philip

Printed at Thomson Press (India) Ltd

For Johannes Laping and
Chandan Sengupta

Contents

Preface

Childhood Repulsion

Your father touches you. As do your forefathers. They touch you with their caste. 'Whose son are you?' 'Which caste do you belong to?' 'But you people are Paramanik, aren't you, barber folk?' … It began right from my school days. Back in primary school. 'No, not here. Your place is at the back, the last bench at the back.' Why? Someone might answer back, but they may just as well not. You simply had to know the answer in your head. You belong to a low caste. You are not supposed to talk loudly. You should not stand with your head raised high. The front bench is not for you.

Baba used to say, 'Study, keep studying, Ratan, I'll give you something if you do well in your exams.' Baba is no longer alive. I myself am approaching the end of my days. My lost childhood beckons me. The day of my *hatekhori*, my school life, my classroom, and my last bench … My friends from my school days who have gone very, very far away from my life, and my teachers as well, all of them keep waving to me as they fade away. My Baba. 'I'll give you something if you study well.'

I never ever did well in studies. But life endowed me with a lot. The school life of my childhood, the casteist slurs—all the memories crawl out together. They look at me and laugh. As if with eyes full of mischief they keep telling me something. As if they keep asking—didn't that childhood repulsion give you any strength at all? Did you get nothing at all from that?

Adhir Biswas
2019

THE LAST BENCH:

AN UNTOUCHABLE BOY'S CLASSROOM

I Was So Happy

Baba had opened the shop a long time back. No customer had come in yet. It was to fetch customers that I was hovering around in front of the Kali temple. If I spotted anyone, I would call out and bring them along. People with long hair and unshaven faces.

Fetching people was my job. If I did that well, Baba would definitely give me an anna. It wasn't noon yet. But the first customer of the day could nonetheless be hailed. Seeing me standing quietly, Baba called me. He said, 'Will you go to Kobiraj Moshai? If you go to him and mention my name, he'll recognise you. He'll give you a bottle of herbal decoction. Tell him Baba will come and give the money after the market closes.'

'I'll go,' I said and continued looking for customers.

But Kobrej Moshai knew me too. Whenever I went to him, he enquired, 'How's your Ma?' 'The same,' I would reply, adding, 'But she was very breathless yesterday.' Or I would say, 'She's just been sleeping for the last two days, I didn't see her open her eyes. She'll get well, won't she, Jaetha?'

No, I couldn't really spot any customers. My eyes were fixed on people walking this way from three directions. As soon as someone came near, I hailed him, 'O Chacha, will you have a haircut? A shave?'

The man walked away without saying anything.

I only stood there on the days of the *haat*, the local market. On other days, it was from the nearby villages that people visited. Most were known folk; they had haircuts on credit. Baba had to cut their hair even if they didn't pay. If he didn't, they would go to another shop. It was better to give haircuts on credit than to be sitting idle—in the hope that they would pay later. But there weren't too many barber shops. Only three that we knew of. Debu-da's, Shyama's Baba's, and ours.

We lived in the same village, and because we were all in the same trade, there was a bit of rancour. I don't mean quarrelling; it was about getting more or less customers. Debu-da's shop was just beside ours. If customers went there instead, I would get angry. But Baba thought differently. He gazed at that shop. Then turned his eyes away. He only said, 'Debu's in luck today!' I would then realise how harsh it felt when the first custom failed to materialise. The others in the trade sat on bricks, near the rice mill. They wet the beard or stubble with water and ran their razor. They charged half of what we charged in the shop.

This marketplace in Magura was called New Market; the old one was called 'the other market'. This market came alive twice a week. On Sunday and Thursday. Ma would push me to go. 'Go quickly, he's all alone, how'll he hail customers when he's working? Go, my precious boy!'

All of a sudden, I spotted a man of Baba's age. He had a bag in one hand, and a basket in the other. He was going to buy vegetables as well as fish. Bottle-shaped baskets like that were for carrying fish. They had a red band around the neck. Yes, it looked like he was coming this way! And, his hair did seem long.

People had passed by earlier, but was that because I couldn't call out to them properly? This time I asked softly and courteously, 'Will you have a haircut, Kaku?'

He stopped as soon as he heard me. Why was he looking at me like that? He asked, 'Will you cut my hair?'

'Not me, my Baba. I can cut nails.'

I thought he was a good man, or else why would he ask me that? It was because he was good that as soon as I touched his hand, to my surprise, this Kaku-person enclosed my hand in his and led me to our shop. Baba looked pleased.

'Master Moshai!' he exclaimed. And then he offered the stool courteously, and said, 'I was looking for you. I'm lucky, the Almighty let us meet!'

'Who's this, Narayan?'

'He's my little son.'

'That's what I thought, who else but your son would call me so lovingly! So tell me, why were you looking for me?'

'Admit my son in school, Master Moshai! After all, he must study, mustn't he?'

'That's very good. Hey, what's your name?'

I felt terribly shy. Hadn't I just asked him about a haircut! Seeing me silent, Baba said, 'Tell him, tell him your name!'

After I told him, it was to Baba that he directed his question, 'Is his *hatekhori* done?'

'Yes. Fatik Thakur did that last year.'

'Then there's no problem. Class I, right?'

'I guess so, he knows to say the alphabet, he knows it by rote.'

'He's such a big boy now and yet you folk don't send him to school!'

'What can I do, Master Moshai! You see we don't know about such things!'

'Then it's Class I. The admission fee is six annas. How much for the haircut did you say?'

'Thank you. It's four annas.'

'So what's the balance then?'

'Two annas.'

'Give me that after you cut my hair today, he'll be admitted.'

I was going to school! A slate. A wet rag. Books, covered with brown paper. I could see everything in my mind's eye … Crossing a river before reaching the school. By a bamboo bridge. The river Nabaganga. The school shed with its thatched roof of *shon*-grass laid over old log rafters. After you crossed the riverside jetty at the bamboo bridge, one had to pay two paise. Students didn't have to pay. And as soon as one passed the pakur tree, there it was, Nanduyali Free Primary School. The bell signalling the end of school. *Dong, dong, dong!*

Baba was taking a lot of time cutting Master Moshai's hair. He was giving more time because I was going to be admitted to school thanks to him. His hair would be cut well. I was so happy that I didn't have words to describe my feelings. I didn't want to go back to standing outside again. When would I start school? Had Master Moshai dozed off? I thought of telling Baba to ask him when he woke up—was it in the thatch-shed across the river that Class I sat?

But even before I could complete my thoughts, I heard Baba's voice. 'Go to Kobrej Moshai. You won't be able to leave once customers start coming.'

The customers had to be told to wait at the bench; the stool had to be extended to them to sit on for the haircut; the change had to be fetched. There was so much work to do. If someone was in a hurry as they sat on the bench, I had to politely tell them, 'Don't leave. Chacha!'

If someone had no moustache and wasn't wearing a lungi, he must be a Hindu. I had to say to them, 'Just wait a bit, Kaka! You'll get your shave right away.' But if the customer got up to leave even after that, Baba would say, 'Wet his beard!' I would do that at once. Apply shaving soap on the brush and slather the foam on the face of the customer sitting on the stool. To tell the truth, he couldn't leave after that. He would think, not much longer now. If he stayed back, that meant two annas for us.

I had thought that by the time I returned with the medicine, the shop would be busy, and that Baba would say, 'Go and dust the towel. Run and fetch change, Chacha's waiting. Go to Wahid's shop and ask him to keep five annas and give change for the balance.' If one had a haircut as well as a shave, it was five annas instead of six. A discount of an anna. But no, there was none of that. Baba was sitting idle. Why was that? After all, the haat was crowded with people. When would the customers come if they didn't come now?

Seeing the shop empty, I had a sinking feeling inside.

Hadn't I told Kobrej Moshai that Baba would come and give the money after the haat? If the shop was empty how would he do that? Had no one come after Master Moshai? Did Baba have change to give them? Would my school admission be on credit then?

Are You Barber Folk?

Ma had asked me to wait a bit. But that had been a long while back! How much longer? What was she looking for inside the room? What was so important now? I couldn't understand why she had asked me to wait! *Oof*, why did she have to do this when I was in such a hurry! Should I leave? No, maybe she'd give me something. Did she go in to get some money? Wouldn't be bad if I got some. After all, I was beginning school today. It was my first day of school. If not an anna, even two paise was good. But I wouldn't wait longer for that.

I could easily run all the way, but because it was the first day, I wouldn't do that. If Ma held me up like this hereafter I would just leave. Hey, why was she going from one room to another? I knew that Ma shouldn't move about like us. That was the toll of suffering her sickness. I saw Ma every day, but I had never seen her like I was doing today. Bustling around for so long. And through all that, it seemed to me that Ma was moving about with her sari wound around her body like thin skin.

Ma had had her medicine. The decoction from the kobiraj. Some pills. A powder. Only after having those did she begin cooking for the household. Baba too lent her a hand. That meant cutting the vegetables, washing them, washing the utensils, and preparing the wheat dough. Sometimes Ma would do it; at other times Baba would say, 'Leave it, I'll do it.' He wasn't around all the time, so he tried to do some of Ma's work in the little time he had at home. But despite all this, why wasn't Ma getting better?

'O Ma, it's getting late. What are you doing? Tell me what you're looking for.'

'What else! The kohl container. It was next to the candlestick. Did you move it somewhere?'

'Aah,' I said impatiently. 'What do you need the kohl for?'

'Oh dear! What are you saying? You're beginning school, won't I put a dot on you?'

'What'll happen if you don't put it? I've grown up now—I'm off!'

'Wait.' I had never heard Ma shout so loud! She wasn't angry, it didn't seem like a scolding either. It was like indulgence. I was annoyed but I couldn't move. Ma walked slowly towards me. Coming closer, and before I knew it, she held my head gently between her palms and kissed me on the forehead! 'Do your studies mindfully, my dear, I'm afraid I won't be there to see it all.'

The thought of school vanished at once from my mind. Why was she choking? As she swallowed, she sniffled a little. Her eyes were brimming with tears. As if she was going to ... just now. I said softly, 'Are you crying, Ma?'

'Where, no!' And saying so, she wiped her eyes. 'Go now!'

What if I went after a few days instead? Or never went at all so I could stay home with Ma? Could I not learn a trade like Baba's instead of going to school? After all, I had gone all the way to Poyatibari after a bereavement there and cut the nails of the people in the household. The womenfolk there had held out their hands so gently. One finger at a time. In return, a clay bowl full of rice.

My mind wandered to that day. Aush paddy was planted in summer and harvested in autumn. Its rice was brown-coloured. Also round potatoes, and sometimes clinking coins. So what if I was small, after all I belonged to that caste. I filled the bag with fistfuls of rice. The vegetables would be placed on one side. But that was for later. As soon as the bag was full, I would hear someone from the household say, 'Don't keep sitting there, come back to the house, come and have lunch when you are done.'

I could see it all, as if Thakur Moshai, the priest, was sitting far away from me. A banana leaf was full of rice, dal and vegetable curry. After mixing them with my hand, I licked the starch off my hand and fingers. Time and again I would think, no one was watching me eating, were they? Oh, how long it had been since I had eaten so well!

In front of Thakur Moshai were Kakima and others of the household. I was served a lot of rice and vegetable curry. It took a while to eat that. Someone shouted out from the veranda, 'Just ask if you want more rice.'

I wondered, isn't there anything else? Some fish? Maybe not the choicest one but perhaps a tail-piece? But then I thought, where's the need for that! With what I had been served I wouldn't have to eat till noon the next day. I continued eating. As I ate, I began to feel drowsy.

So, what was wrong with that—if I went around from village to village with a nail-cutting chisel? I could start earning right away. I just wanted to stay close to Ma. I wouldn't go to school. What if she kept on crying after I went to school?

Ma understood. There were tears in my eyes. She wiped my tears and said, 'Go, my dear, it's getting late.'

I didn't say 'no'. Once again the urge to go to school awakened. 'So, I'm going!'

Ma nodded.

I had come quite a distance. But Ma was still standing on the road in front of the house. I turned back every now and then to look. Ma waved her hand.

Chhor-da had left already for the day. Ma had said to him, 'Drop your brother at school tomorrow.'

'He'll go on his own. Why are you worrying? He wanders around everywhere all day long; won't he be able to get there?' he had said.

Baba too had left for his shop quite early in the morning. Mej-da was sleeping. Bor-da had left for his in-law's house.

As it is, my brothers—my dadas—didn't venture to the shop. They were ashamed that Baba did this to earn a living. Chhor-da's friends teased him, calling him 'barber'. He didn't like it but couldn't say much in reply. I too knew that if I said anything to them rudely, they would smack me. They called me that too, 'Hey you son-of-a-barber, you blackie ...'

My dadas made sure to walk at a distance from where the shop was. I didn't feel bad at all that no one was going to drop me to school. Why would I, after all I went everywhere on my own. I knew all the places! There was Ma, still standing. Once I turned at the curve in the road at the banyan tree, I wouldn't be able to see her any more.

A shanty. It had no walls. Nor a fence. Just posts on four sides and a tin sheet on top. That was the school. The cemented floor was chipped and broken in places. Everyone had sat down leaving just those broken parts vacant. The room was almost full with the band of students. I wondered where I would sit. I looked here and there. There was such a clamour! I couldn't fathom anything. It was Class I, wasn't it? Was I even in the correct classroom! Was anyone from my village here? I tried to identify them. Where did Sir sit? As I was about to enter the classroom, I heard, 'Ratan!' Who called me?

I entered. Who had called me? The students were like a shoal of squirming fish. Who was it?

Everyone had a slate in their hands. And a wet rag. What was the book in their hands? The same call again, 'Ratan!'

'Hey Dulal!' I said, and smiled. Did I say that too loud? Everyone turned to look at me. Dulal was the son of the sister-in-law of Punyo Majhi, from the riverbank. Not exactly from my village, they lived at a little distance from the banyan tree. He was my marbles playing companion. As soon as I began to hover outside his house, he knew that I had come to play. We made a clearing somehow in a wooded part and began playing.

Baba had come to recognise Dulal. If he ever spotted him outside our house, he would come charging and hit me hard. Baba only had to say, 'Marbles again?' Just that. And if Chhor-da heard that, he too came charging and—sometimes the thrashing left me with a bleeding nose or lip. But it was when Chhor-da, who was strong, hit me that Ma got frightened. Even if she couldn't get up, she wanted to ward him off with all her strength. She would want to restrain him. And if Baba was there, she would weep, 'Oh dear, you hit him so badly, I'm going to lose Ratan! Hit me instead …'

Dulal would run away hearing the sounds of thrashing and weeping. It was the same Dulal. He asked, 'When did you get admitted?'

'Yesterday, at the haat. When a Sir came for a haircut.'

Dulal knew that the Master admitted students outside school as well, in the market, or at a shop. He didn't want to know any more. He said, 'Sit down. Sir will be here in a little while. When he calls out your name, say "Present Sir!"'

The boy beside me asked, 'Where do you live?'

'You know the banyan tree, if you go a bit beyond that, you'll come to a house with banana-leaf fencing, and a threshing hut slanting askew beside the road. With bamboo supports. That house. Isn't Sir going to come?'

'Oh he'll come, he'll be here. Where's your book?'

I was silent. Had Sir said anything about that?

A boy wearing pants torn at the backside slid towards me. He said, 'I think I've seen you somewhere.'

'Was it at the shop?'

'What's your shop?'

'A barber shop.'

'Are you folk barbers?'

The boy was bare-bodied. I was looking at Sir's chair. The broken handle had been fixed with a string. I also noticed a boy with a dot of sandal-paste on his forehead. Was he also a new student like me? The other boy suddenly grabbed my shirt. And then he said, 'Why aren't you telling me?'

I was in Class I. Back in East Pakistan, the hatekhori ceremony used to be carried out in Hindu households once a child crossed five years. The days had flown by since then, it had been a year or two. And now I was admitted to school. How old was I then?

I was scared. Would he hit me here, inside the classroom? Why did everyone hit me? Was it because I was dark-skinned? Or because I went to other people's houses to work? Would they have let me join their games if Baba were not in this line of work? Would I have been spared the beating? Perhaps it would have been best if I hadn't come to school today. How tearful Ma had been.

Seeing that I wasn't saying anything, Dulal retorted, 'Is cutting hair bad? Can you go around without having your hair cut? My uncle catches fish, which he sells in the market. Is that bad work? So why do you think of caste?'

The bare-bodied boy was not a little but much bigger than me. Then Dulal said, 'Come, Ratan, sit here.'

The field in front of the primary school was very green. The schoolhouse was south-facing. It was Dulal who told me, 'Once we're in Class II, we'll go to that nice schoolhouse.' The clamour was gradually coming to a close. He said, 'There's Sir!'

'But I know him. He walks along the riverbank. He's from Atharokhoda village. That's the village directly across from our village jetty.'

'Can you see that, just look, that's the register. Your name's in that. Do you remember what to say when he calls out your name?'

'Pejen Saar!'

He patted me on the knee, and said, 'Correct!'

Sir fastened the string on the handle of the chair before sitting down. Did he know what had been happening here just a little while ago? The boys who were saying nasty things had also become like wet cats all of a sudden. All silent. Suddenly Dulal took my hand and held it to his pocket. 'Can you feel it?'

Marbles here too! I suppressed a laugh. He pressed his finger over his lips. 'We'll play a few rounds after school gets over.'

'But I didn't bring any'

'You're an idiot, I wonder why you're such a coward! Always keep marbles with you, I'll give you some, so you can play if you feel like it. Hey, it's your first day today, didn't you bring any money to buy snacks?'

I nodded to say no.

Dulal looked glum. He said, 'You could've bought some marbles with that money, played a round with that …'

'Oh heck!'

Then I said softly, 'I think Ma would have given it to me if I had asked. But she was crying then.'

'But why was she crying? Did you say something nasty?'

'Oh nothing like that, it's just that her health's getting worse. She thinks she's going to die. Thinks she won't see me anymore. That's why.'

Sir began calling out names. We were talking furtively. I wouldn't have mentioned this, it was Dulal who suddenly asked. Besides, he was the only one I knew here, and I had only whispered it to him. He was about to say something when Sir said, 'Who's that talking?'

Several of the students turned around to look. I looked at them blankly, like a good boy. As if to say, it's someone else who's making trouble, not us, Sir.

After looking at us briefly, he continued calling out names. As soon as he called out the last name, 'Ratan Paramanik', I sat up, startled.

It wasn't anyone else, was it? My heart was beating fast. He called out my name again.

'Ratan?'

As soon as I raised my hand, Sir asked, 'Will you say something?'

'It's me … I'm Ratan Biswas, Sir.'

'When did you get admitted?'

'Yesterday, at the haat.'

'Who admitted you?'

'A Sir, the one who's dark-skinned. A bit plump. He had come to the shop for a haircut, it was that Sir.'

'Then it's you.'

'But we are Biswas!'

'That's fine, what else could your surname be but Paramanik? Sit down!' And saying so, he closed the register.

What a Wretched Cracked Mirror!

Baba squinted his eyes and examined the hair at the back of the head. He wouldn't notice even if someone were to stand beside him. He didn't notice that I was there, nor did he realise that I had entered the shop. I called him softly, 'Baba!'

He raised the pair of scissors from the head. 'Could you learn properly? Sit. Just a bit more. Can you lift up the curtain at the door? It's not sunny anymore.'

Baba ran his eyes over the hair for the last time. Then he turned to me. 'How many books need to be bought? Have you written everything down?'

On good days when there were a lot of customers for haircuts, there would be clumps of hair all over Baba's dhuti. It was my first day at school. Baba had been busy. I could lend a hand now if there was any more work at the shop.

Where on earth had Dulal vanished from the bridge, he didn't say a thing! He had only said, 'Go now!'

The customer was looking at himself again and again in the mirror, turning his head at times. Leaning forward, he said, 'Can you hold the mirror at the back?'

Baba was moving the small mirror to show him the back of his head. This side and that side. 'Hey, hold it properly! Why are your hands shaking?'

'Here you go!' Baba said solicitously.

'Raise the mirror!'

Baba would have held up the mirror even if the man had not jerked his head like that! 'Did you get hurt—'

'What a wretched cracked mirror you have!'

Baba was silent. He felt bad at such admonition. If only he'd asked me instead of Baba …

The man was very annoyed. But should he have flung the coins? Baba picked up the change carefully. He didn't say anything. He simply took it in. All of it. He examined the coins to see if they were in currency. As he looked at them, he asked me, 'Did the Master Moshai ask you what you learnt?'

Just as I had felt bad for Ma while leaving for school, I felt the same way for Baba now. I kept gazing at him. He couldn't see well. Ma knew that customers didn't want to go to him because he was old. If I went along perhaps there'd be a couple more customers.

Baba had an incision scar running from the middle of his chest to below his navel. His abdomen had been cut open at Calcutta Medical College Hospital for a digestive ailment.

Baba removed his spectacles and wiped his eyes several times. 'Did you write down the names of the books required?'

Why wasn't I able to reply? Why was I gazing at him blankly?

I kept gazing at him. I remember an Urdu-speaking man had made Baba a pair of spectacles. It wasn't just Baba, several people in the marketplace had them made. The man had sat all day under the jackfruit tree beside the Kali temple. I remember more—when Baba returned home, Ma had gazed at him for a long time, as if it were some stranger who had entered. 'What happened, my dear, can't you recognise me?' Baba had said.

'I'm just looking.'

'What are you looking at?'

'At the new person. With new eyes.'

'I got the spectacles made. I was scared … what if I cut someone while running the razor over their face?'

'Can you see clearly now?'

Baba didn't reply at once. After a pause, he said, 'It's clear, but it's also hazy. A lot of things suddenly appear large. That's the only difficulty. It'll be fine. After all, anything new has to be hazy for a while.'

Baba still had the same pair of spectacles. He didn't wear them for long. He said that he couldn't see clearly with them. He could see the marketplace and the people clearly when the shop was empty. He merely wiped his spectacles from time to time. Wiping them now, he said, 'Do you want to eat something, Ratan?'

I wanted to, I could go and fetch something. 'Like *singharas*?'

'Will you get that at this hour?'

'Shall I go to Makhan Kuri's shop and have a look?'

'Go. Get some if it's available. Tell him my name. One for you and one for me.'

On credit yet again! I wanted to ask him, why buy on credit all the time, Baba? I don't want any if there's no money! But I couldn't say that. It was the first time he had asked me to buy something for him at the mention of food. Baba wanted to have it too. So, babas too liked to eat, just like us!

As I ate the singhara, I suddenly envisioned Ma trying to step down from the veranda, holding the post. She was unable to get her feet on the ground although she was trying to. She held on to the post. Baba asked, 'Hey, what's up, why did you stuff it all into your mouth? What's the hurry?' No. It couldn't be said. Not even to Baba. If I did, he'd say, eat slowly. Finish eating and then go. But I didn't have to say anything. Baba understood, I was going back home.

The marketplace was desolate now. Only a few people were around. Just as one went past the Kali temple's jetty was Orey Kamar's smithy. It was really snug there on wintry days, and he could be seen bare-bodied in front of the fire as he hammered away at iron. Needless to say, he didn't wear a shirt in summer. In fact, I had never ever seen Orey Kaka with a shirt on at any time of the year. He pumped the bellows holding the string attached to the handle. He held pieces of iron in the fire using tongs. There was a dog sitting in the shade of the door-flap of his shop. It was sleeping with its face snuggled into its side. It had other friends and companions in the marketplace. Most of them clustered around the food shops. The way they gazed at you. They said so much with just their eyes … such entreaties! They just looked longingly. They didn't bother you if you didn't give them anything.

Once the lotus-leaf wrapper was thrown away, they licked it on both sides. That was all.

I had taken only a slate to school and a wet rag between my fingers. I was taking all that back. There were a few shops on the road from the market; on the left side was the jute warehouse. This was the way to our house. The tin-sheet walls of Murari's hut. The grapefruit tree. And then written on a wall with tar-paint 'Sadhana Aushadhalaya Ltd Dhaka'. I gradually arrived at the wooded part full of trees. The river Nabaganga lay on the right side. I advanced.

I didn't look back because this was a familiar route. Besides, I was in a hurry. I had to go back home. If I had turned around to look, I'd have seen the doorways of the shops hazy in the distance. I wouldn't be able to say which shop was ours from so far away. I wanted to go home. The way I had visualised it while eating the singhara—was Ma walking a bit now? I began running. Did I drop the rag? Who was this man? Was his house in town? Near the cinema hall? Was he a policeman? I held the slate to my chest. Oh, I was breathless! But it wasn't very far now! There's the banyan tree.

What was the sound? Was it the bell ringing? I halted. But as soon as I did, I remembered. Ma.

Did Baba know the Master Moshai? He was so much younger than Baba. Did small boys talk to grown-up folk like I had done? Did anyone hold them by the hand and pull them like that? Ratan Paramanik. It's me, Sir, Ratan Biswas. It's a barber shop that you have, isn't it? What else would your surname be but Paramanik, boy? Sit down.

The door of our house was open. No, there was no fear. No one entered our house. That's why there were no thefts either. Theft meant cutting through the earthen base and entering, and then taking the utensils and jewellery and scooting. The thieves knew it was pointless going to this house. Only Rani, the neighbourhood cat, entered the house, hoping to pilfer something to eat. After going around a bit, when it didn't find anything, it sat at the door. Was it because it got nothing here that it gazed at Ma? She was lying down. The cat went away.

But so what if it went away, it was a devil, it would come again the next day. Look around again. Gaze at Ma again before leaving … what did it see? I spotted Rani as soon as I stepped onto the veranda. *Hei!* I shouted. It knew well that this driving away was only feigning on my part. Rani got off the veranda in her own time.

I was about to call out, 'Ma!' How long had she been sleeping? Baba had told me, 'Never call her when she's sleeping.' I heeded that too. When I placed the slate at a slant against the bamboo-mat wall, it fell down. I pressed it down with both my hands, as if to muffle the sound. No, even that didn't wake Ma. I left the slate on the ground as it had been.

I tip-toed so that I made no sound. Ma didn't hear me. I went closer. Why was her mouth gaping like that? Her eyelids were slightly open, a bit of her pupils were visible. Let her sleep. Baba had told me not to wake her up.

The rods at the window were made of strips of date tree bark, the windows of wooden planks. That's where the room got its light from. And ventilation. So many tiny flecks of dust were visible in the band of light coming in now. Tiny fleas floated in it too. The sun gave some light to the room late in the afternoon. It stayed for a little while. After that the sun would take that bit back and leave. I observed all this as I lay. No, there was nowhere to go today. I would stay indoors. I would stay with Ma. I could never be with Ma except at night. Wouldn't my dadas return home? Let them not return until Baba finished at the shop and made his way home. I would get up after that.

I had done all this furtively, so Ma had no clue. She had no idea when her Ratan came in and lay beside her.

I don't know when I dozed off. 'Wake up, my precious!' I woke up as soon as her hand was laid on my head. I heard the sound of conch shells blowing in the neighbourhood.

Ma said, 'Get up now!'

'No, I won't!' I snuggled against her and asked, 'What's our caste, Ma?'

'Did you go to the shop?'

'Is Paramanik the name of our caste?'

'Why? Did someone tell you anything?'

'The Sir in school gave me this name. When he called my name, he said "Ratan Paramanik".'

'Let it be, whatever Sir thought was best … Many of our folk have that name.'

'That's why I didn't tell him anything.'

'That's good.'

'Why do you sleep so much? Do you feel terribly sleepy?'

Ma laughed.

'Don't sleep all the time. I get scared.'

She pulled my head to her bosom. She said, 'What would you understand, my precious!' And then she added, 'Listen to your Baba. Listen to your dadas. The way you get thrashed when you don't listen to them, I get scared! Someday I'll hear that …'

'What'll you hear?'

She pressed her hand to my mouth. 'Wait a bit, come let's light the lamp. Conch shells are being blown in all the households, let's do that too.'

'No, it'll be difficult for you, Baba said not to do it.'

'Your dadas didn't continue their studies, but you've started going to school now. It's an auspicious day for me!'

I knew that the conch shell was kept at the same place where Ma had looked for the kohl container. At the little shrine. With a picture of Goddess Lakshmi. I picked up the conch and tried to blow through it. It made a bit of sound but that was all. The moment she tried to take it away, saying, 'Not like that', I too said at once, 'You mustn't blow it at all! You don't have to blow the conch for anything auspicious. I'll be fine without all that.'

The Wick Full of Pus

After a good night's sleep, I was awakened by a kind of indistinct sound. Like brushing, accompanied by the melodic chant '*Bhajo Shri Gourango, Prabhu Nityanando*'. Baba was sweeping the courtyard with a palm-leaf broom and singing the *naam-kirtan*. Baba woke up every day before dawn. Did one sleep less as one grew old? Or did he wake up so early because of worries? He ran the broom over the messy courtyard. He sprinkled dung-water. He also sat down to cook a bit of rice. He had to rise early if he had to do all this. It was as if the new day crept in holding Baba's hand. Once it was morning, Baba used to call out from the courtyard itself, 'Ratan, get up! Dulal, get up! O Sukumar! Are you up?' Dulal and Sukumar were the names of my Chhor-da and Mej-da.

Sweeping the courtyard, washing it with cold water, Baba did that all by himself at dawn. He didn't even have a shawl over him. Just his thin dhuti. Didn't he feel cold at that early hour of the morning? Apparently, he didn't. He didn't listen to anyone either. And who would tell him? It was Baba who did the telling all the time! He had something to say to everyone.

Do this, do that. Didn't I tell you yesterday to go to so-and-so, did you go?

I could figure out what Baba was doing even as I lay in bed. My sleepiness loosened its grip on me with the sound of the broom. He called out again. I could tell that Baba was getting annoyed. So I got up. Wasn't he talking to someone? Who's come?

'Why do you ask me about Ratan? Go and have a look, the *laatsaheb* is still asleep.'

'Still asleep?' Ashit echoed, and entered the house. As if he had got permission to go in.

I saw him and shut my eyes at once. But he jostled me and asked, 'Won't you go to pluck flowers for the Hyanchra pujo? Rabi and all have already gone!'

'Let them.'

'We'll go near the riverbank. You know what, Ratan, they won't get even a quarter of what we will. Come, get up now!'

'Where are you doing the pujo?' Ma asked.

'Under Apu's bel tree. I've made nine mounds at its base. That's where the pujo will take place,' Ashit said.

Ma was sitting with her back resting against the bamboo mat wall. Baba had laid out a makeshift mattress there using old *kanthas* and rags. She couldn't lie on the cot. She was very ill. She had been ill for a long time. Her stomach was swollen. I pressed her feet the other day, and my fingers sank in. 'Does it hurt, Ma?' She shook her head. 'No, it doesn't hurt.' Was Ma telling the truth? But it wasn't like that for me. If I pressed my feet hard, it did hurt. So what was Ma's illness? The old aunties in the neighbourhood murmured, 'Ratan's Ma is terribly sick.'

There were various pujos throughout the year. In winter it was Hyanchra pujo. This pujo was performed by children. Because it was children like us who were most affected by it. Scabies, itching. The Goddess of scabies, Ma Hyanchra, was pleased if this pujo was performed. If she was pleased, she wouldn't afflict you with scabies and itching. Ma didn't say anything when she heard the name of the pujo. After all, I was scratching myself all day. As soon as Ashit mentioned plucking flowers for the pujo again, I sat up with a start. Baba hadn't scolded Ashit either about plucking flowers so early in the morning. He pulled my arm again. He said, 'Come now, hurry up and come … Hey Ratan, I heard you joined school yesterday?'

'It's very cold outside. Do something, bring your Dada's old shirt that's hanging there. I'll put it on you,' Ma said.

'Doesn't he have a shawl, Khurima?'

'I'll tell your uncle to buy it. Let him wear the shirt for now. Your shawl's a nice colour, dear.'

Ashit was pleased. 'I bought it from the town after all.'

I wore the shirt, but the sleeves hung loose covering my hands completely. Even my fingertips weren't visible. The shirt was too long as well. It went down to my knees. It looked strange. Sensing that I was grumbling inwardly, Ma said, 'Go on now, who's going to look at you at this hour? You're going to the woods to pluck flowers, so it doesn't matter if anyone sees you. Everyone knows your father's poor.'

It was lovely at this early hour. It had been a long time since I stood at the riverbank this early. The water was calm. The Nabaganga looked like a road stretching out till far in the distance.

The winter breeze was usually mild, but it was absent at this time. The tiny fish on the river's surface looked almost mist-like as they swirled and leapt about, unable to rise very high. After all, they never enjoyed such desolation! As the day advanced, there was the clatter of utensils being washed. Big boats went by, pulled from the shore. They had to flee then and hide. That's why the small fish were playing to their hearts' content now. Leaping out of the water with glee. I thought about all that as I looked.

Ashit advanced along the riverbank. Hadn't he noticed that I had stopped? It was best if he hadn't. Let him go. I liked standing here. It was so cold on the way here from home. But it wasn't as bad here, in front of the river, was it? It felt more like the last few days before winter departed. Neither hot nor cold. 'Hey Ratan, what are you doing?'

'I'm coming!' And saying so, I left the sandy bank and walked ahead. Along the undergrowth.

Bor-da had said, 'Go and meet Nuro today. I studied in the same class as him. He'll know who you are once you mention my name. Just tell him that Kalidas Biswas is your Bor-da. If you tell him you're my brother, he'll be kind to you.'

'Who's Nuro, Bor-da?'

'You silly chap, don't you know him yet? Your headmaster.'

'What does he look like?'

'I don't know what he looks like now. It was a long time ago! He used to wear shorts back then. His hair used to be backcombed. He is short.'

'Yes, I've seen someone like that. He's our headmaster.'

'Why're you calling him "he"? Refer to him respectfully!'

'I've seen Sir.'

'Yes. You must address grown-up folks respectfully.'

Nuro Sir was the headmaster. Bor-da ran a shop. The shop didn't do so well either. And because it didn't do well, he went and returned as he pleased. As if he had no attachment. Why had Bor-da, Mej-da, Chhor-da—all of them discontinued their studies? I had heard that Mej-da, Chhor-da, my elder brothers worked as clerks in shops. Why hadn't my dadas continued their studies? Till which class had Bor-da attended school? Which school had he attended? Was it our Nandol school? Did the Sir who was his friend live near town? Or in some nondescript village? I could remember a bit. That Sir came to the school on a cycle. A cycle would be parked near the staff room. So that was the headmaster's.

The names of my books were *Kochipata*, *Dharapaat* and *ABCD*. I liked reading *Kochipata*. *Dharapaat* wasn't bad either. Everyone read out tunefully. 'One moon. Two cycles.' And so many pictures in the book. When one held all these books to one's nose they smelt nice. Just like new clothes smelt good.

Chhor-da put covers on my books. He had pasted the paper cover, made from bamboo-leaf, so well that it wouldn't tear unless one pulled on it very hard. But the slate had fallen from my hand the other day and cracked. It didn't come off because it was fixed to a rectangular wooden frame. I didn't tell the folks at home about that. If Chhor-da found out, he would kill me.

I was very scared of him. Bor-da and Mej-da, not so much. Only Chhor-da. I kept the slate under my books all the time. Only I knew it was cracked. When I was asked to write something in school, I did that. As I wrote, the letters kept getting divided. Sir didn't ask to see, so I didn't know what he would say if he did. It was best that he didn't see my writing for as long as possible.

I didn't go to school every day. I didn't feel like it. Sometimes while walking to school, if there was no one around, I slipped into the woods. I kept my books at the base of a tree and covered them with dry leaves. After that I would peep, like a jackal before it crosses a road. No one had seen me putting the books down, had they?

Whenever I felt unwell or had a fever, I would go and stand in front of Ma. When she touched the back of her hand to my forehead, it meant she would say, 'Let it be, you don't have to go to school.' If she said that, it wouldn't matter even if I had a fever.

I would then play near the house itself. Even if my dadas spotted me, they couldn't say anything. I would tell them, 'Ma told me not to go.'

'Why?'

'I have a fever.'

Seeing my appearance, Chhor-da would be surprised. 'Let me see.'

Like Ma, Chhor-da too felt my forehead with the back of his hand. 'Don't you learn even after being thrashed?' But he didn't say any more than that. I was saved.

Playing meant playing by myself. No one in the neighbourhood really played with me. That's why I spread out a sackcloth and sat by myself. Playing shopkeeper. Come in, Dada. Eat it while it's fresh. *Danadar*. *Jilipi*.

Did winter only bring in cold? No, it also brought scabies to the village. It was almost like a winter playmate. How could it get left behind? That wasn't possible. It would definitely come. Scabies wandered around at will during winter. Of course, it kept itself concealed. It searched for households that were poor. Households in which people wore old clothes. Possessed only a single set of shirt and shorts. If those were washed there was nothing else to wear. It looked for the susceptible bodies of children from such households.

If winter was a person, I would definitely say to it—come alone, if you can, or else you needn't come at all, summer's just fine for us. We had to perform the Hyanchra pujo because one couldn't say that. There was no way one could sleep peacefully at dawn. Flowers had to be plucked. Whoever wanted to offer flowers to the goddess had to pluck it themselves. The flowers would all have disappeared if one was late.

I know that our kanthas were dirty. Our clothes were dirty too. How much could Baba do? In other households, soda would be added to water and boiled in a tin can to wash the linen. In our household, they were only washed in water. Who could do more? Ma would ask us to put the things out in the sun. That was all. No more. I think scabies liked to set up home only amidst dirt.

The scabies turned restless as soon as one stepped out into the sunlight. It called out from under one's pants to be scratched. To tell the truth, that felt really pleasurable! As if it would be nice to scratch other places too.

It felt blissful the moment one's nails touched the spot. One began to feel drowsy, bit by bit. After a while, I would go behind some concealment and look, and get scared at once.

Blood. And a white liquid oozing. Much more of that than blood. Large scabs. All over the backside, on the groin. One was scared to take off one's pants. Would the sore get infected? I couldn't walk. It hurt when my pants grazed those parts. I walked with a crooked gait. And thus did I go to school.

Pus had been oozing out of my left ear the last few days. The other day Ma had put me on her lap, made a slender wick with the end of her anchal, and drained out such a lot of pus! Every time she put it into my ear, it came out wet. She put it into my ear and twirled it around. I shut my eyes in pleasure. Aah!

'Why do you jump around in the river and get water in your ears, Ratan? You'll become deaf!' Ma kept twirling various parts of her sari. After the end of the anchal was twirled around inside the ear, the pus-filled cloth emerged like a straight, slender wick. If there was a delay, I gripped her hand and put the wick back inside my ear. 'Put it in!' I would say, hurrying her. There was nothing else that was as pleasurable as scratching the inside of the ear with a cloth wick.

It had been quite a while since I had started going to school. Everyone knew where I lived, and what Baba did. I didn't have nice clothes. Just my books, the wet rag and the cracked slate. As if everything about me was visible. These people had figured out everything. It was only Dulal who spoke to me at times. But in the midst of conversation, he would remind me, 'Did you get marbles?'

But I was always scared. What if someone heard about the marbles and complained against me to Sir? I gestured to him—we'll go near the rice mill and play. He didn't understand my gestures. One day, after staring at me silently, he asked again.

In the midst of all this, the boy sitting beside me suddenly screwed up his nose and asked, 'Isn't there a terrible smell? *Oof!* Can anyone smell it?'

The pus-filled wick. I wanted to pull my Ma's hand each time and smell it. Was it that smell? But that didn't seem rotten to me. I sat up straight. I tried to be a good boy. As if it weren't me, and the smell was from somewhere else.

The others snuffled. 'Yes, there is some smell!'

'Did anyone fart or what?'

'No, it's not a fart smell. It's like something rotten ...'

And then everyone sniffed around. Someone nearby said, 'It's coming from him, smell him and see!'

'Yes, you're right! Hey, what's up, didn't you wash yourself after shitting today?'

I was trapped within their talk. 'Of course, I did!'

'Then? What's the smell?'

It was time to turn silent once again.

'*Oof!* How dirty your clothes are! Doesn't your Ma wash your clothes? How can you wear such smelly clothes?'

The boy who was slightly big, the one who spoke on every matter in class, came and began smelling me. I sat inert, not moving. It was like cockroaches were sniffing me from all sides. Smelling my body. Smelling my head. Suddenly someone pushed me and shouted out, 'I found it! The fucker's ear's rotten!'

'Hey Habib, throw the bloody son-of-a-barber out!'

The boy came rushing from his seat near the chair. Even as he advanced, he said, 'Get out, fucker! Go and clean your ears first!'

Another boy said, 'Let it be, leave him alone. Better to make him sit at the back.'

I never sat in front after that. One day, as the names were being called out, as soon as I said, 'Pejen Saar', Master Moshai asked, 'Why are you sitting so far away?'

That big boy stood up and said, 'His ear's rotten! His clothes stink. We asked him to sit at the back, Sir.'

'That's good.'

Pleased with himself, the boy glared at me before sitting down again.

My head was lowered. I could visualise my Ma. As soon as I reached home, she would call me. 'Come, let me clean your ear.' I walked slowly, taking one step at a time. And as I walked, I imagined myself lying down. Ma pulled me to her lap. And then, inserting the wick into my ear …

What Had I Said!

One night Baba said to Ma, 'Go for a visit to your folks in Ramdebganti. I'm telling you because you're better now. You haven't been there in such a long time. And after you return, I'll go as well.'

'I don't feel like it any more. I don't like to see their poverty. The same hardship from my childhood till now. From what Bor-da told me, I think …'

She then said her horde of nephews would come running to her. 'What can I give them? So many bellies to feed from their tiny *paan*-yard! And if I then land up there too …'

'You're right,' Baba said softly.

Ma had been looking at him and listening. His words weren't trivial. Yet she said, 'I had gone to attend Boudi's *sraddha* ceremony, that was a long time ago. I haven't been there after that, that's why I was saying …'

'Now that you are a bit better, take Ratan and go. He keeps talking about his Mama-bari.'

'It's not that I don't want to go. But he's started school. I know they want to see their youngest nephew.'

'Why don't you go? After all, it's your own house. Sure, they have problems. But you haven't been there in a long time, and given your health, who knows what might happen …'

Ma was quiet for a long time. Why was she silent? What was she thinking about with her head bent down?

Baba then promptly said, 'Shall I inform Nilu? He can come with a horse-carriage. Come via Rajpat on your way back. You can take the launch and come to Nandol. To Teermuni ghat. If you go, do that on any day except Sunday and Thursday.'

'Don't I know? It's because Ratan goes to the shop that you get some work. Who'll call the customers if he's away? You know the other gems … I wonder what they're ashamed of! Anyway, if I do go, I'll skip those two days.'

Thank God I was nearby. 'What did you say? Mama-bari?' I kept tugging at Ma's arm.

'Let it go, dear, you're tearing my arms out!' As soon as I left her arm, she said, 'I'll die if I take you along. I know that if you go you'll spend all your time at the riverbank. I took such a lot of trouble to remove the pus from your ears.'

'No, I'll be with you all the time!' And I ran off. Past the village boundary, past the persimmon tree, along the cane field fringing the lake. It was a holiday. I wouldn't go to school today even if Chhor-da thrashed me!

The school was off on Fridays. During the summer, Ma would ask me to sleep in the afternoon. But if I had to sleep, that ought to be beside the lake. Where would one find a place like that? Straight ahead from the lake was the tamarind tree belonging to Rabi's family. In summer, the neighbourhood folks carried a mat and pillow and went there to sleep. They gossiped there. They wove date-palm mats as they sat in the pleasant breeze. The grass had become flattened with all the people sitting on it. The area under the tamarind tree, carpeted with fallen leaves, was like a soothing, cool mat. The lake was a little distance away. In fact, there was a small lake and a large one too. A huge one. Washed by that, a breeze blew across the paddy fields and the ashsheora wood. It blew one's hair away. I wanted to let Ma know that I was going there. I hadn't slept. I didn't feel sleepy in the afternoon. I didn't sit with the people who gathered there either. If I did, I would have to hear annoying talk. They talked about one's caste. Sometimes they said, 'Hey blackie! Whose house did you eat in today? Hey look, the barber's gorged today, see his swollen belly!'

Did I ever run to eat anywhere? I only went when I was asked to. After all, I only went to the households where they asked me to clear the garden. Did I go around the village crying, 'Do you have any work?' I didn't do that! I only went because they asked me secretly. Folks at home thought I had gone out to play. They didn't look for me. They only did that if I wasn't back home at night. That was convenient for me when I went out to work.

As soon as I arrive for work, they show me the place and hand me a spade. Nothing more. But does a spade suffice for everything? Undergrowth, grass, vines and creepers. I steel myself and clear all the undergrowth. If I get a basket, I can do it quickly. But I can never dare to ask. Finally when the work is done, I say, 'Khurima, I've finished.' But no, it's not over even if I say so. They come and have a look to see whether everything has been cleared properly. Only then. If it's even a bit untidy—'What's up boy, you've learnt to skive even at this age?' After that is lunch. With fish, occasionally. It's fine even if there's none. As long as I get plenty of rice. After all, they only provided food. So why so much talk about that? Ashit too does the same work. It's only the two of us from our village. If grown-up folk do the work, it's three taka a day. Because I'm still young, it's only lunch.

I don't like all that talk. And then I think, after all, the village doesn't belong to anyone. As it is, I don't mingle with anyone. I only go to the lakes in summer because I feel like enjoying the breeze there. It's fine as long as I don't sit with the other folk.

I sit amidst some ruins atop a small hillock. There were acacia and date trees. It used to be someone's homestead. Very old. We don't know who the homestead belonged to. We only know it as Kutibari. Full of undergrowth. Apparently, the hillock is a den of cobras. So what, after all I wasn't going to harm them. I fly a paper wheel. The wheel spins in the air. I hold the stick in my fingers. Lots of thoughts crowd into my mind. Except for Bor-da, my brothers aren't doing anything. That's because they didn't finish school. Mej-da goes off somewhere from time to time. Ma weeps. No one can tell her of his whereabouts. And for as long as there's no news of him, Ma just keeps weeping. She says we ought to visit the shaman at Nakol. She asks Baba to go there and get him to divine his whereabouts.

But Baba retorts saying, 'Let him perish!' Why does he say that? The moment he says that I visualise Mej-da's dead body. He looks like he's sleeping. His eyes are half-open. Gazing affectionately at Baba. Why do I see that?

One day I saw Baba hitting Mej-da. As he was being hit, he gripped Baba's arm. Baba was unable to free it, try as he might. Since then he seemed to be ever more annoyed with Mej-da. Was that why he said, let him perish? Those glistening waves. The waters of the lake. A clump of water-hyacinth. Nowla fish nested beneath that, and if one moved away the hyacinth and plunged one's hand in, there were singi and magur fish. Let the rainy season come.

It was Sache-da who taunted me the most. He didn't like me going to his house.

I didn't know his name all these days. I only knew him as 'Sir'. Entering the classroom, even before calling out the attendance, he said, 'Bring a container from home tomorrow. You'll be given Dalda and milk.'

After he said that, the boy in front of me asked the boy beside him, 'Shall I bring a bottle for the milk?'

'Ask Satish Sir.'

'No. He's said it once. What if he asks, "Were you sleeping?" if I ask again? What will I say then?'

'Then keep quiet. It's no big deal. He asked to get a container, so get it. I'll bring a platter from home.'

'And what'll you get for the Dalda?'

He said something or the other, I couldn't hear it all. I sat at quite a distance from these boys. That's why I couldn't hear their whispered talk.

For a long time I wanted to tell the big boy in my class, smell it, there's no pus in my ears. Ma took it all out with a wick made with her anchal. I had washed myself thoroughly with soap-nut too. But I decided not to. The moment I saw his face I dropped the idea.

Did I really stink? But I had never got any trace of that. So many customers came to Baba's shop, wouldn't they have reacted if I really did stink? They would definitely have cried out, 'Hey you boy, get away, you stink!'

Or did the boys make me sit at the back because my clothes were shabby? Or because I was a barber-boy? Or did someone say something to that big boy? I couldn't figure anything out. Let it be, I hadn't told Ma about any of this either. There was so much she wanted to know when I got back from school. 'Did you fare well today?' Sometimes she said, 'You must teach me to write letters once you get to the next class! I'll learn to read from you. I'll learn to write. And then I'll write a letter to your Boro-mama … won't you be able to teach me?'

Ma had such hopes. It wasn't easy for me to speak about those things to her. She said so many things … wishing the best for all of us. When she got an asthmatic attack, it looked like her eyes would pop out. She couldn't think of speaking then. She cried a bit, but not very much. Sobbing as she cried. I couldn't tell Ma that I sat right at the back. And because I sat at the back, Sir didn't ask me anything. He didn't ask me to write anything either. I just wrote down whatever Sir wrote with chalk on the blackboard. I never went and showed him what I wrote. Because the letters got severed on the cracked slate. It was just as well that I didn't have to show him. I wouldn't be able to say that my new slate had cracked!

Because I sat at the back, no one asked me to do any tasks. Like fetching water. Or picking up a fallen piece of chalk. The girls were called so they would pluck out the new grey strands that sprouted on Sir's head. So they could pluck out each one of them. I had been sitting at the back for almost a year, and I had never been called for anything. Whatever Sir taught, my lips repeated. Whatever he asked us to write, I wrote. Like in the village, I was under boycott in school as well.

I knew I'd find the pot as I was setting out from home. Bottles and suchlike were kept near the elevated platform. But I could just not find the real thing, that pot. It was getting time for school. Perhaps the bottle that was used to keep the mustard paste, *kashundi*, would suffice for the milk. Who knows how much milk Sir would give! The pot would be just right for the Dalda. If they gave just a bit, that was fine, and if they gave a lot, a potful was no small thing. I used that pot to bring the prasad after the Narayan pujo. The potful of prasad was enough for everyone. It would hold quite a lot of Dalda as well. But where on earth was it?

I rushed towards Ma and asked, 'Ma, where have you kept the pot?'

'What do you need the pot for?'

'Does one have to tell you everything?'

'Why are you being like this?'

I thought I'd keep it a secret. I would bring milk and Dalda from school and surprise her. It was the first time I was going to bring something home. How could I disclose that in advance?

I looked again. Kept looking. There were sounds of various things falling. Ma asked, 'Why don't you say what you need it for? You're going to school, so what do you need the pot for?'

'Not just the pot, a bottle as well.'

She was quiet now. Maybe she was thinking about something. Not finding the pot, I asked again. 'Can't you remember?'

'I can't get up. But wait, let me try.'

'You don't have to do that, stay in bed. Why don't you talk of dying, I can see that death's standing close to you!'

I didn't even feel like looking at Ma's face. She didn't say a word after I said that.

Did Ma say anything? I couldn't hear her.

What had I said! But I still wanted to search for the pot. No, I didn't want the milk and Dalda at all. *What had I said!* What kind of talk was that! Could one take one's words back? Why was I feeling so strange? Why this sudden rush of feeling that made me want to cry?

As soon as I opened the door at the rear, I began my long run. So that no one in the village could spot me. No one. I wouldn't return home. I would return after Ma wept and searched for me, like she did for Mej-da. I was running. 'Hey there! Why're you running? Is Khurima ill?' I didn't reply to Shyama. O Ma don't die, I said it by mistake! I just kept repeating that to myself.

The place was far away from the Nandol school. Near the river Madhumati. No one would find me in this unused spot. The river water glistened in the sunlight. Our Nabaganga flowed into this. I can't remember how long I sat there. Had the Dalda been distributed in school? The milk? Did everyone get a lot? I had heard that it was given twice a year. All this came from abroad. They also gave clothes for poor kids. Would my name be left out because I was made to sit at the back? After all, we belonged to the ranks of the poor. And then it suddenly occurred to me that if one ever uttered something wrong, there was a way of making it go away. You went waist-deep into water, repeated what you had said, and then made a cross mark on the water.

I descended at once to the water of the Madhumati. 'O river water, I asked Ma to die, take those words back.' I said that three times. And each time I implored, 'O river water …'

Dulal Had Come to Play

Our household had been in ruin for a long time. One frequently heard the word 'ruined' in the village. It was mentioned more by people like my Ma-Baba. Who did that refer to? To someone who had no oil in their hair, and didn't have proper clothes. A person who remained silent. He was the one who was ruined. He had lost all attachment to his household.

What if a homestead gradually became like that? If there was no one to look after it, wouldn't that too be 'ruined'? A house that wasn't swept and mopped. Where weeds grew until it was a jungle. Where mosquito eggs hatched in the water accumulated in an earthen pot, and larvae glided here and there to their hearts' content. Where the bamboo roof supports were sagging. Perhaps if they hung like that for long, the roof would eventually collapse. Wasn't this homestead ruined too? I asked Ma about that. But she then asked me in turn, 'Where did you learn all this talk, boy?'

'We are the poorest in the neighbourhood. No one likes a poor household and poor folk, Ma!'

'What happened? Did someone say anything to you?'

'No, who'll say anything? Sometimes I feel bad for you all. How hard Baba works to earn a few paise. If only you were well … I wonder when I'll see you smile. See you talking happily.'

'Am I not smiling now? Let it be,' and at once Ma tried to laugh, tiredly. 'You don't feel bad now, do you?'

Ma pretended to laugh. I could spot that. It wasn't just in this instance that Ma concealed a lot of things. She lied on our behalf, and said nice things even to Baba. I did so many wrong things, but she never complained to Baba or my dadas. Why was that? Did everyone's Ma conceal complaints on their sons' behalf? I went close to her and said, 'Can you rest on my shoulder and walk, Ma? Come on. Let's walk a bit in the courtyard!'

I was helping Ma walk. Were her legs kind of limp?

Ma walked. But she didn't walk this way earlier. With me right next to her, resting on my shoulder. 'Here Ma …'

She had got the sari that she was wearing during the *sraddha* at Atharokhada. It was an affluent household. After the heads of the two sons were shaved and they had taken a bath, their dhutis were given to us. Apparently, the two dhutis left behind at the riverside were our due. Baba asked me to wring the water out of them. Could I twist them around like Baba and get the water out? I used not just my hands; I pressed them against my chest too. Why were the dhutis smelling bad even after they were washed with water? Was it because they hadn't been washed in a month?

But all my unhappiness vanished when I saw the rice and potatoes laid out on gamchha in front. And paan leaves and areca-nut. Taka-coins placed over that. All for us! The father of the shaven-head boys said, 'Narayan, I got the sari for Bou-ma.

Take that along too. And make sure both of you come on the day of the *sraddha*. I won't go again to invite you.' Now who wouldn't feel happy to hear that!

That same sari. The one with a red border. Ma looked like the Kola Bou, or ritual consort, placed beside the image of Ganesh on Durga Pujo, a small banana plant draped in a red-bordered sari. My dark-skinned Ma looked nice too. After walking a bit, Ma said, 'Shall we sit for a while, my love?'

'There's no need. You've walked enough. Come, let me take you to the veranda steps, you can sit there.'

As we walked, I kept noticing her leg hanging limply. Her feet were getting entangled again and again in the red border of her sari. Ma seemed to get back her composure after sitting on the veranda steps. Soon after, she said, 'Ratan, why were you making such a fuss about the pot the other day as you were leaving for school?'

'Let it be, you don't have to hear all that.'

The month of Ashwin followed Bhadra. It had been a few days since Baba started going not only to the shop but also venturing far outside the village for work. The houses of people with jobs were close to the town. He set out at dawn, and then returned to open the shop. Baba had said that it was getting difficult to run the household unless he earned more. I think he had been thinking about that for a long time. And since he set out at dawn, he could no longer do the house-related work.

The soil in the courtyard was covered with earthworm droppings. It was full of leaves, not just from our guava tree but also other trees nearby. One could also feel a slight chill in the air at night. The coming of such a time meant that Durga Pujo wasn't far away.

I thought I had spotted Dulal walking in front of our house after a long time, lost in his own thoughts. He cleared his throat and said something or the other, and then stopped. I went out, and it was as I had surmised. As soon as he saw me, he ran behind the mango tree for cover. It was I who called him back, 'Baba's not here. Wait a bit!'

'I was scared. I thought your Baba was about to—'

'No, Baba left at dawn. That's why I could come out. We'll play only a few rounds today. I won't buy any more marbles if I lose. My exams are coming. Baba's told me I have to do well. He said he will buy me something if I pass.'

'What will he give you?'

'I didn't ask him, but when he's said he'll give it, he will.'

'You're right, Ratan. There's no need to play. I've got to study too. My uncle has said that he'll drive me out if I fail.'

This was the first time that Dulal was worried about exams, like I was. He said, 'Come, walk with me till the banyan tree, and you can turn back after that.'

I had never had a conversation like this with Dulal before. Playing marbles gave him another kind of delight. And now Dulal was turning down that delight and walking away. I was left with a bad feeling. He had come with such hopes. He had stood up on my behalf so many times. If a fight broke out when we went fishing, he came in between. It was the same in school. The same Dulal had come to play now. As we walked, he suddenly held my hand. Would he not come again?

He wasn't one to eschew words. He gripped my hand in his fist. He said, 'I'll go home once the exams are over. It's been such a long time. I won't return. My Mesho won't keep me any longer, even if I pass …'

'Why are you saying that? Your Mesho will surely call you back once you're promoted to the next class, just you see.'

'No, Ratan. We are four brothers and sisters. We are very poor. Mesho kept me in his house for so long on Ma's request. I've lived in your village for a long time. After all, I have to go back one day.'

I could have let go of Dulal's hand now. My heart felt heavy. But I didn't have to let go of his hand just because he had loosened his grip. I was in tears! Like the way I was in tears after telling Ma about dying, and I went and sat quietly at the desolate place by the river Madhumati.

Dulal went away. In a little while, he was a hazy image in the distance. Or was it my eyes?

Not for once did I think of wiping the tears brimming in my eyes.

The Horse

No one had forbidden me from going to the Durga Pujo pavilion last year. I stood with everyone and saw the idols being made, using frames fashioned out of shon grass. After the sound of the knocking of each bundle of dry stalks of shon-grass on the earth, as Tinnath Pal tied them together with string, he laid the dummies down beside him. He then fastened them tight, holding them upright between his legs. Saraswati. Kartik. If there was a twisted trunk, I recognised it as Ganesh. Everyone figured out that the Durga idol was larger than the other ones. When a fat dummy was made, that was Asur Moshai! Everyone gathered below the banyan tree then. One didn't feel like going to school. You wished you could be around Pal Moshai all year long. Until the idol-making was finished, Pal Moshai slept in the Durga pavilion itself. He only left thrice a day to have his meals at someone's house. The children of the households took him along. I really wished I could call him to our house to eat. He was invited by one house and then another in rotation. We were the only household excluded. Was it Baba who had spoken about this exclusion? Or was it the Kakas organising the pujo who had told Pal Moshai that we wouldn't be able to feed him? Had they said that we were low-caste? That it was improper to eat in such a household and then make Goddess Durga's image?

Pal Moshai had been in our village for a long time. He arrived from Rajpur, which was near my Mama-bari. After preparing the dummies, he would apply one coat of clay and then return home. Those were left to dry at the Goddess's pavilion. The ten arms of Goddess Durga were held together in place with string. Almost all the idols were ready till the neck level. It seemed they would be completed in a couple of days from now. After that came the painting of the eyes, using the oil from gorjon tree and peacock feathers. I stood and watched, and wondered. We would never get to invite this person who made such beautiful images of the gods and goddesses. Once the idols were installed in the pavilion this time, I would offer pranam and pray—make Ma well. We'll invite Pal Moshai for a meal next year. Ma will cook for him. Rice served on a banana leaf. I would serve him water and salt.

But Pal Moshai wasn't worried about food. He knew that having come here to make the idols for the community pujo, he would go by turn for his meals to one house and then another. The pujo organisers also gave him the beedis he required.

When he suddenly found he had none, he could just tell one of the kids, 'On your way to school dear, tell Dulal Kuri that Pal Moshai has no beedis.' He only had to mention that. If I had heard that, I would run and get it for him. Giving it to him with one's own hands meant you were a secret intimate of his.

But why were my friends not allowing me to go into the pavilion this year? Did they know that Baba would give only a tiny donation? Did they know that we wouldn't feed Pal Moshai? They did know that I wouldn't get nice clothes like them. But was that the reason for being forbidden to enter? It was the first time I saw a rope in front fencing off the pavilion. Of all people, the kid Nitai had entered. I was pushed away the moment I went there. Someone said, 'Hey, stay outside. Dulal Kaku has said not to let in those who don't donate bamboo poles. You don't have a bamboo clump! Go, stand outside and watch!'

Straight ahead from the Pujo pavilion, at a slight distance, I was clearing the banyan leaves and making a place for playing marbles. Not to play with anyone, I would play by myself. Pick up the marbles. Aim and strike. I didn't have many marbles. After Dulal left that day, I didn't buy any. I didn't play marbles with anyone else either. I don't know why I brought them along in my pocket. Besides, I hadn't seen Dulal either for some days. Why wasn't he going to school? Did his Mesho really drive him out? Or, was it that he had heard such talk and left on his own for his village? Whom could I ask? Who would be able to tell me about him?

I sat with the marbles spread out in the space I had cleared. No, no one was coming to me. No one said anything to me. All the cheer was in front of the pavilion. If only Dulal's house had been in our village. If only Dulal would come now, play a few rounds with me, and then leave if he wanted to. I say, wasn't there a school in the village he belonged to? Weren't there weekly markets? If Dulal's was a slightly well-to-do household, I would have asked him: will you take me along? I'll do all the housework. I can do everything. I'll study in the school in your village and play with you. Once in a while I'll come back to my village and meet Ma.

Pal Moshai was erecting the straw dummies of the idols in their frames. Wasn't that one the dummy of Ganesh?

'Who's that? Oh, you!'

It was Budho's Ma.

'He won't take the marbles! He'll just shake them a bit and give them back again. Do you know, he can't speak. But he torments me to death. He just points his finger and indicates, take me to the banyan tree—and so I brought him along. Will you play with him for a while, Ratan?'

'Let him play. I'm here, aren't I? He'll be alright.' And then I said, 'What's up, Budho? Want to play marbles?'

He put down the marbles, clapped his hands, and said, 'Ba-ba!'

One had to go past Chhoto Mama's house to get to Budho's place. Keep walking, and after going for quite a while through the woods, one came by a hut with a thatch roof. That was Budho's house. His father, Kaka used to take the horse carriage along that path. A thin and small horse. Looking at it, you would think the horse was fever-ridden. Rheum in its eyes. Flies buzzing around it. Kaka never rode in the horse carriage. Perhaps he thought it would be difficult for the horse. He used to load sacks of paddy and bundles of straw on the carriage and walk alongside, a riding crop in hand.

After Kaka died, I went to his house. He lay on a kantha spread over straw. Did people's bodies shrink when they died? Sunlight filtered in through the greenery. So many people had come, even though the house was in the woods at the end of the village. And then to the crematorium. People had gone to fetch dry jute stalks and wood. Would the wood for his pyre be carried in Kaka's horse carriage? Did the horse know? It was tied to an areca-nut tree. There was no fodder in front of it. Perhaps no one had even noticed it. Everyone was only talking about Kaka. The horse was completely silent. I went closer and looked at it. Someone said, 'Hey Ratan, move away from its legs, it might kick you.'

I moved away. But I didn't tell it anything. Would it kick even if I didn't say anything? But if someone in the house you had come to for condolence told you something, you had to listen, right? I didn't stay there for long. I stayed there just for a little while and then left. Did Budho remember Kaka? He again said, 'Ba-ba!'

I saw Budho's Ma holding the reins of the horse and feeding it grass. Sometimes, as she fed it, she came towards us. Dirty clothes. Prickly hair on her once-shaven head. Budho was wandering nearby. Striking plants and leaves with a stick, he looked happy. He kept uttering 'Ba-ba'. He had no siblings. Now it was only him and his Ma.

Did God love to live in poor households only? Budho's Ma begged for a living now. She went to distant villages, taking Budho along. 'Didn't you go out today, Khurima?' I asked.

'No, son. I don't go every day since the horse will be left all alone. Like with Budho, I'm worried about him too.'

Budho's Ma talked about so many things with a small boy like me. My Ma too didn't really have anyone to talk to. Budho's Ma had said, 'If I go to any neighbourhood, everyone assumes I've come there to beg. That's why I don't go anywhere. Will you keep Budho company for the few days of the Durga Pujo? Will you take him around and show him the idols?'

'Yes, Khurima. I'll come and fetch him. The two of us will go around and see the idols. We'll go to see the idols under the Baidya household's bakul tree in Atharokhada.'

'You've saved me, Ratan!'

'You go, Khurima, I'll take Budho back.'

'Oh ... you saved me!' Budho's Ma said once again. And even before she could finish, I sought her indulgence. 'Will you give me your horse?'

Budho's Ma was startled. 'What will you do with it?'

'It'll stay in our house. I'll take it out to graze. I'll play with it.'

'*Dhur*! Does anyone play with animals! You have so many friends in the neighbourhood!'

'No, Khurima, they don't play with me. No one is friends with me.'

'So does that mean—?'

'Give it to me! Tell me, will you?'

Budho's Ma was thinking.

'Once it comes to our house, it'll stand still as soon as I start caressing it. I'll wipe it clean with coconut husk. I'll remove the rheum from its eyes. I'll bathe it carefully. So that no water enters its ears. Or else it'll get pus in them, like I did. Khurima, do horses get pus in their ears?'

Budho's Ma burst out laughing. 'Who told you that?'

'So you're giving it to me then?'

This time Budho's Ma didn't think at all. 'Just grow a bit older, dear!'

'I got it, you won't give it to me!' And saying so, I held Budho's hand and walked towards the pavilion. Nitai wasn't around now. Let's stand in front and watch the dummies of the idols being prepared.

My Name is Ratan

Two people were standing near the ticket booth at the narrow bamboo bridge. All the others went their own way. I was going across the bridge. As I neared, the boy said, 'The Pujo holidays have begun. And we'll be in a new class after the exams. You had to sit at the back because of Wahab, Ratan. Just you see, he won't be able to pass the exams. Once you're in Class II, you can sit in front.'

'Can you recognise us?' the girl asked me.

'I do.'

'Our Baba is the priest who performs the Durga Pujo under the banyan tree in your locality.'

'So you're Kalpana!'

'How did you know?'

'Because when Sir calls your name, you say "*Pejen Sir*". I can see everything from the back.'

It was the first time someone from school had spoken to me nicely. I had observed that she could correctly answer everything that Sir asked her. Their names were Swapan Chakraborty and Kalpana Chakraborty. I think they were siblings. I couldn't think of anything else to talk about. We stood there for a little while, and then I said, 'I've got to go home.'

'Alright, go!' they said.

Thanks to Goddess Durga, I had become acquainted with two people from school.

Pal Moshai's house was near my Mama-bari. In Rajpur. The Rajpur that was close to the jetty from where Baba had asked Ma to board the launch. I could have asked him whether he knew my Mama-bari folk. I didn't get the chance to do that. But they were just not letting me enter the Durga pavilion. That was mostly Nitai. He was the one driving me out. We lived in the same neighbourhood. But he had suddenly stopped recognising me. He had been given the responsibility of permitting only selected people to enter the pavilion. And that had suddenly made him feel very officious. Let him do that. My day would come too.

If I got the chance to talk to Thakur Moshai, the priest, before the pujo commenced, I would tell him that I was in the same class as Kalpana and Swapan. I would tell him that they had told me about him, and so I had come to speak to him. If he needed anything, he should only ask. I would be around nearby. He just had to wave his hand, and I would be there. Or he could call me by my name. My name is Ratan.

Although the holidays had started, I didn't feel like going to the banyan tree. I went a couple of times to meet Budho. He came along with me one day. But after a while, he kept asking for his Ma. He held my hand and took me towards his house.

When I went there to drop him, I found that Khurima wasn't home. Where had she gone? To beg? I was very worried. There were no other houses nearby where I could ask. I brought Budho back to the banyan tree. It was almost evening by the time his Ma came there to pick up Budho. I told her, 'Budho was crying a lot for you.'

'I knew that he wouldn't be able to stay away from me. Still, you did a lot dear!'

'You'll give me the horse, won't you?'

Coming closer, she kissed me near my ear and whispered, 'Just grow a little older! You can take it when you can hold the reins and feed it grass.'

'How much older? When I'm in Class II? Or Class III or Class IV?'

'It's you I'll give it to when you're educated and grown up.'

Budho kept tugging at his mother's hand. He was drooling from his mouth. 'Ma,' he was calling out.

There was only a solitary road going along the river, with bamboo thickets on both its sides. The clumps of tall trees had already cast the road in semi-darkness. The idol-making in the pavilion wouldn't go on for much longer. The images would be painted in a few days. The work continued through the evening, under the light of Petromax lamps.

Perhaps Budho would not come again. His Ma would take him along when she went out to beg. I could have explained so many things to him had he been around. Not that he would have understood everything. But at least he would listen to whatever I said. Would his Ma take him along even on the days of the pujo?

It had started becoming chilly at dawn and dusk for the past few days. Earlier everyone at home used to scold me and coax me to sit and study. But lately they didn't have to say a thing. I lit the lamp and sat down to study on my own. As soon as I opened the textbook, *Kochikatha*, all that was written inside floated into sight. The light of the kerosene lamp fluttered. I looked at all the text, one line after another, in that light. I could remember everything. If I was asked anything, I would be able to answer. I could write it out as well. Kalpana was good at everything. After having asked me to sit at the back, Sir never remembered me on a single day. Would I have to sit at the back on the day of the examination as well? How would I be examined?

There was a narrow path beside our house. Adjacent to that was a large pit. There were only persimmon trees along its edge. Of all the trees, it was these that the bees had selected to make their honeycombs on. These persimmon trees had the only honeycombs in the village. There were no other trees near the pit. And the whole area was wooded. The pit filled up during the rainy season. Shol-fish and tadpoles darted around in it. And it was from that pit that one would suddenly hear the sound of frogs being caught by snakes. *Chaon chaon.*

The main road lay in front. Would anyone say anything if I sat near the pit in the morning and read my textbooks? Perhaps not. It was a public road. And so I laid a sackcloth and sat down. I read out tunefully. I had never heard anyone being told anything for reading aloud. Meaning, I wasn't doing anything wrong.

Not being permitted to read out loud because I belonged to a low caste wasn't the case either. On the contrary, seeing me studying, Baba had proudly announced at home at the top of his voice, 'Go and see how mindfully a boy from a poor household studies!'

The sound of my reading grew louder. As I read, I observed the drops of dew on the blades of grass. Sunlight crossed the tin roof of Gour's house and fell on the grass. I continued reading. I didn't look in any direction. I had to do better than even Kalpana and her brother. The other day, Baba had said, 'I'll give you something if you pass the exam.'

When Baba said he would, he would certainly give it. But I had no idea what it would be.

A QUIET AFTERNOON

Where It's Sunny

'Will you go somewhere with me?' Ma asked me.

'Where Ma?' I asked in surprise and went close to her.

'Where else can it be? Let's go somewhere nearby. Where it's sunny. I'm feeling cold.'

'I'm shivering too. Shall I change my clothes?'

'Do you want to? Alright, do it. But we're not going to visit anyone. Just for a walk in the sun.'

'Shall we go to the metalled road?'

'That's too far away … what's the point in going there? You know I'm not well.'

'We could see the motor bus. It makes a terrific sound when it runs. If the driver sees us and stops, you'll be able to see how people travel by bus to visit their in-laws.'

'Do you like getting on a bus?'

I laughed and nodded my head. 'Yes. A money bag on the conductor's shoulder. *Ichhekada! Haor!* That's what he shouts out to pick up people. I saw that when I went to Mama-bari. He bangs on the side of the bus when someone has to get off.'

We latched the house door and were on our way now. There were so many trees on both sides. We wouldn't get any sunlight unless we left the hamlet.

'Why would the motor bus stop? Even if many people stand there, it doesn't stop unless you wave your hand. After all, we aren't going anywhere,' Ma said.

It felt strange. That we were outside. Ma was always indoors. Everyone went to this house and that house, but I had never seen Ma going anywhere. No one came to meet her either. I was so happy that she wanted to go out today. So let her go wherever she wants, I wouldn't say anything. I would just walk with her.

We went past Anil Kaka's house and the persimmon tree. Menfolk sat and gossiped and smoked hookahs in the shade of the tree, while children played *danguli* and marbles there. We walked towards the ruins. In the course of the conversation, Ma said, 'Can one leave an empty house and go anywhere, silly! Thieves roam around during the day too.'

Ma wasn't wrong, thefts were a common occurrence. One would be woken by the sound of screaming. And then hear that thieves had dug their way inside such-and-such a household and stolen everything. Whatever little was there was—all gone. One even heard of plates being stolen, leaving the householders without anything to eat from. I went to see for myself with my rheumy eyes. I found a crowd there. The thieves had indeed worked hard to dig a hole through the earthen plinth. There had been no sound because they had used sharpened spades. As they cut through the earth, the bamboo-prop at the base hung loose. Didn't the people have any clue? Were they so fast asleep? I asked Ma, 'Why are you afraid? What do we have at home?' There were only a few utensils. We didn't have any bell-metal plates. No brass pots. I made a joke. 'Your thieves know very well how wealthy we are. Even if they dig their way in and enter, all they'll find inside is a tattered kantha.'

Ma said, 'Even so, whatever's there isn't insignificant!' Then she added, 'Aren't there some fruits? What will you sell in the market if those are stolen? What's the point in going far when you know that?'

Bunopara was a short distance away. We went past the Kutibari ruins and were nearing Pireni Ma's hut. After that came Bunopara, where people would ask, 'Hey dear sister, where are you going?'

Small wattle-and-daub huts. With a single door. And a window or two made of wood and bark, supported with laths. With drawings of men with bows and arrows on the wall below that, and of a wild boar fleeing. A mother winnowing paddy on another wall. As if her fingers were moving the winnowing tray up and down, *tokas tokas*. I walked slowly holding Ma's hand, and observed everything. Such tiny huts, and yet so neat. All plastered with cow dung.

Ma suddenly cried out, 'Look at the shimmering water, Ratan! No one gets into the water past noon, that's why it's so still.' And then she said, 'Look, the kite's caught such a big fish! What fish is that?'

'Sorputi.'

'Are you sure?'

'Then what? What else could such a big, white fish be other than sorputi?'

'You're the one who can see well, you have sharp eyes.' Then she said, 'Let's sit for a while beside the lake. It's nice and sunny here.'

If one looked beyond the algae and hyacinths on the surface of the water, there was a large garden full of greenery. It was as if someone had meticulously woven this green wood. Seen from afar, the green wasn't exactly green since the village was wrapped in mist. I was observing and thinking about all this. Was Ma taking it all in?

Was she without a *ghomta* because no one was around? One never saw women in the hamlet without a ghomta. They left their heads uncovered only at home. Ma too. The moment she stepped out, her hand moved to the anchal on her shoulder. To put the ghomta over her head. But there was no one around now other than me. Was she looking at the water in the lake? Or something else as well? Apparently, people gazed like that when they were in anguish. When grief flooded one's sight. Is that what Ma was seeing?

The gentle sun had taken away the cold from our village. The soft sunlight warmed us. It made one feel cosy and drowsy. I looked at Ma again. Why was her face like that? As if she had been angry with Baba and then walked a long way after that. And then come and sat down all alone. With her Class II son. I knew that she had no one else who would listen to her. And where on earth would she go leaving me behind. That's why I was with her. But I wasn't happy. Should I pat her? As I observed the water, I noticed a wonderful grasshopper on the stem of a water hyacinth. It had donned so many colours! The grasshopper circled around; it was never still. It looked this way and that, darting its irises. What was it looking at? It seemed to be very happy. What did grasshoppers eat?

I descended slowly to the bank. There was no jetty on this side. Ma suddenly cried out, 'What are you doing? Why are you going to the muddy slime? There are leeches there!'

I didn't realise that. The mud at the bank was crusted at the surface, and the moment I stepped on it my leg sank in till my knee. Ma feigned anger and said, 'Go and wash your legs in the cold water now, you rascal! See the fun!'

Ma held my hand and led me back. I didn't go near the grasshopper; it was afar. I couldn't see it now. I had wanted to catch it by the tail when it dozed off after looking this way and that and then became still.

I would have caught it too if my leg hadn't sunk into the slime. I would have taken it home and tied a length of string to it. And then let it loose. It would play around as it wished. Hopping from one branch to another. Hopping on the marigolds. I would feed it tiny earthworms and ants' eggs. I really wanted to see it eating. But the muddy slime at the lakeside didn't let me do that.

Ma took me to the jetty. She held up my pants, and washed off the mud. The water was very cold. She said, 'You're a real menace!'

I observed Ma's hands as she washed my legs. Her thin arms with the iron bangle. Was the conch-shell bangle on her left arm even recognisable? I felt angry with Baba. Was a pair of conch-shell bangles so expensive? Dark brown mud on the grooved bangle had made it unrecognisable. One could only make out something thick and brown-white. Hey, hadn't Ma mentioned the fruits? I wouldn't give her all the money from selling the guavas and coconuts. I would keep some of it aside. I would say that was all I got. Did they sell conch-shell bangles at the weekly market? I surveyed the market in my mind. No. But there was a shop near Sonapatti, the goldsmiths' quarter, beside Madhumati cinema hall in Magura town. That's it. I wouldn't say anything to anyone. No one would know.

Ma had bent down to wash my legs. I felt like laughing seeing the sari wound over her back. I did something. I stuck my finger into a zigzag tear in the sari and moved it in a circle. As if I was making a large 'zero'.

'What are you doing, you're tickling me!'

'Ma, how many saris do you have?'

'Why?'

'Just like that. I'll buy you a nice sari with leaf and creeper designs on it when I'm a bit older. And I'll set up a shop in the haat.'

'Do I have that in my fate? Will I live that long?'

I removed my hand with a jerk. 'Come, you don't have to bother so much about me. You only say nasty things!'

Ma slaughtered me every day. 'I'll hit you on the face with the broom!' 'What a relief it'll be when you die!' 'I hope I never see you alive again!' And various other things. Did I need to live? Was one supposed to heed Ma's words? Did she really mean all that? Would she have taken me along for an outing if she really wished me harm?

I was returning home holding her anchal. Having come out with Ma today, I felt like buying a lot of things for her. I had never thought about all this before. Why was that? Ma really didn't get anything for herself. We asked Baba for so many things, but did Ma ever do that? I don't think she did. And then I thought, how would Baba be able to do that? He couldn't even earn enough to purchase a seer of rice. I never saw Baba looking happy. He would return home from the market, put down the rice and vegetables near Ma, and say, 'Do you know, Charu, people don't come for haircuts and shaves like before … what should I do … whatever God has in store for us …'

Fortunately our trade did not require us to buy anything. A razor, a pair of scissors, a comb and a sheet of cloth sufficed. I don't know about Baba, but I inwardly prayed to God to keep the rain away during the day. No one would come to Baba for a haircut if it rained. Let it rain at night. And it shouldn't be too cold either. No one would get out from under their quilts and head towards the marketplace if it were cold! I don't know whether God heard me or not, but I prayed for that every day. With my eyes shut. As I stood below the Kali temple. Or anywhere else, but always inwardly.

One had to climb up quite a lot to get from the jetty to Bunopara. I heard the sound of pigs being herded on our way back. No, I didn't hear that. Were they running inside my ears then? Did one hear only with one's ears? Not the mind? *Hui haw! Ho aah! Ririri ah!* Which of these houses did that boy live in? The one who was like me. With the drawstring of his pants hanging out. He was dark-skinned like me. After taking the pigs out to graze, he leaned against his long, bamboo staff and watched them feeding on taro, snails and earthworms. What was his name again? Arey, I keep forgetting!

'Can you wait a while, Ma? I'll just be back!'

And as I said that, I darted between the houses and reached the end of the hamlet. There was a toilet encircled with a gunny sheet in the middle of the garden. Similar to the one in our house. The pigsty was across a pit. Gosh, so many pigs! Is this how they grunted? Was it because of me? It would have been good if the boy was around. He never spoke to anyone when he went through our hamlet with his herd of pigs. He didn't even lift up his head and look. There was only the sound of his cries, *Hui haw! Ho aah!*

No one in the hamlet viewed him kindly. He belonged to a low caste. Ate dirty stuff. How dirty? Why did he eat that? I didn't know. The place was so nearby, and yet I didn't know the name of anyone there. I hadn't seen him in school either. If I had spotted him, I would have told him, 'I had gone to see where you lived.' I would have told him, 'Will you take me along one day?' The pigs would feed in the jungle of taro. I too would cry out, *Hui haw! Ho aah! Ririri ah!*

Ma called out to me. 'Hey Ratan, where are you?'

So many tiny piglets! Their mother was lying down. Was it asleep? They were wriggling as they suckled on their mother's teats. And bumped their little heads against her belly. Didn't that wake her up? Was their mother like my Ma who never said anything? I stood quietly at the edge of the pit. Gazing at them suckling and bickering playfully. Seeing me, a little girl came up to me. She looked as if she hadn't had a bath in a long time. She said, 'They're drinking milk.'

I could hear Ma calling me. I didn't say anything, just patted the girl's face and ran off.

Why Did They Hit You? Did You Do Something?

They hit me all the time. Although I hadn't done anything. They played, but they wouldn't take me. Even if I went to fetch their ball, or the *danguli guli*, they said, 'Hey, don't touch it you son-of-a-barber!' I would just stand quietly. I knew the ball had fallen somewhere in the undergrowth. Because I was standing apart, I had observed where the danguli guli had fallen. But I wouldn't tell them. They searched. I imagined that after a while someone would cry out, 'Look near the base of the assheora tree, you'll find it there!' But I wouldn't say a word. What if they hit me for saying that! 'Did someone ask you to open your mouth?' It wasn't just the beating, they hurled casteist slurs at me. Did boys in other villages also utter casteist slurs when they spoke?

I stood far away and observed them. They would surely find a pretext. Even if they didn't hit me, they would definitely abuse me. I knew them. But I would forget, and go again. I don't know why the sound of boys playing seemed to pull me. The banyan tree and the haritaki tree near the girl Apu's house seemed to call out to me!

That's where my friends played. After all, you called them friends when you lived in the same village and the same hamlet. They were my friends even if they didn't let me join their games. I know they didn't think so. Let them! I would be by myself. I studied. I would work in people's houses too. Hey, didn't I work in the houses of Dipu and Robi, cleaning their gardens, plucking areca, and gathering greens for the kitchen? I had taken a load of paddy to the rice mill and got it threshed just a few days back. And it was Dipu who then served me rice on a banana leaf. He took such care of me! 'Here, eat as much as you can.'

I couldn't figure out why he behaved one way at home, and then changed when he was in the company of his friends. It made me very sad. I felt like hitting them too sometimes. But I couldn't. Was that because I was scrawny? Or was it because I was afraid that their mothers wouldn't call me for work if I hit them?

It happened a few days ago. Parimal was walking in my direction. He was short but sturdy. He didn't have protruding ribs like me. Even his neck was fleshy. He simply had to watch the new movie running at the Madhumati cinema hall every Friday. Parimal was in Class VI. He was good at studies. Not just him, but everyone in his house. His Dada studied in college. No one in the village was as educated. If Baba had admitted me to school earlier, I would have been in Class V by now, if not Class VI. But seeing Parimal approach me, I knew he would do something.

Had I done something wrong? I couldn't recall. Even if I had, I couldn't remember that so quickly. Let's see what he does, why should I be afraid all the time? As I was thinking along these lines, he came right up to me. 'Did you steal our grapefruit?'

I stepped back a bit. 'But that was last year. I plucked just one and ate it.'

The other boys burst into laughter. *Hee hee.* Parimal pounced on me and lifted me up. He banged my head against a sharp bamboo lath. Everything went dark. When I reopened my eyes, I saw that the place was empty. No one was there. Blood ran down my whole body. I wiped off the blood with my hand. I ran my fingers over myself and felt for the gash.

I sat under a small jackfruit tree. No, I wouldn't go home right now. Ma would get alarmed if she saw me bleeding like this. She would weep. If Baba found out that I had come home with a gash on my head, he wouldn't listen to anything. He would just hit me with whatever he found close at hand. I pressed my hand over the left side of my head with all my strength. The bleeding seemed to have stopped. The blood on my hands ran down my arm and accumulated in the fold of my elbow. I sat there for some more time with my hand pressed on my head.

I thought I ought to go to Parimal's house. I would go and stand in the courtyard. Perhaps seeing me covered in blood, they would want to know what happened. 'Hey, who hurt you?' I would then say, 'Parimal hit me.' Would his father beat him? If you cut through their compound, someone or the other from inside always stepped down to the courtyard and asked rebukingly, 'Why are you cutting through our house? Is it a road?'

That was what we did when we had to go somewhere in a hurry. Only a few houses in the village had fences. We cut across those that didn't. But not everyone rebuked us like that. Parimal's Dada would chase me off the moment he spotted me. So it was best not to go there. Wouldn't I get some ground turmeric somewhere? I would apply that to the wound, so it would heal. Let me grow up a bit, after all I was only in Class III now! Let me be a bit older. I wouldn't get beaten up like this then.

There were no houses nearby. Whose house could I go to? What if they reported it to Ma? What if they went to Ma, and said, 'O Ratan's Ma, come and see, your Ratan's cut his head and is bleeding!' It was better to be alone. But I was feeling drowsy! Why was I feeling so sleepy? I felt like taking a nap. Like one felt before a long sleep. Let me wait a while, I would go to the jetty and wash the wound. Would Ma detect it even if I cleaned it up properly? I could see Ma hazily in my mind's eye. She was wearing the same sari that was torn in the back. 'Ma, look, I'll sell our guavas and buy you a sari.' Baba would be stunned. S-t-u-n-n-e-d!

I don't know how long I sat there. It was just before dusk. A red glow had spread over the greenery. It was twilight under the trees. The sun looked like it were the moon. It was about to depart the village. And shortly after that, it would take away the colour it had spread over the land and the sky. Once it did that, our village would be in complete darkness. It was already dark under the trees. I spotted a couple of fireflies. Which bird was it that flew by with a *kik kik* screech? Did they have tiny chicks in their nest? The gambolling of the bats in the bamboo grove of the fairies had begun. There, an owl had cried out too. *Bood-bood-bhu-tu-m!*

Blood had accumulated in the fold of my elbow because my hand was pressed over my head. Did that happen because it had been bleeding for a long time? The colour of the blood was like that of the oil from the hilsa fish. It was my own blood. Red-black. Actually, if one got scared then one was scared, but if one didn't, it was nothing. I would go to the riverbank now.

Was I finding it difficult to get up? Not exactly, but I think I felt a bit giddy. Why was that? Because I hadn't eaten? But why? After all, this had been my routine from childhood itself. I should go. It would get dark if I stayed any longer. Ma didn't let me go to the jetty after dusk. Apparently the water in the river was asleep then. It ought not to be woken up. But I had to go! O Ma Ganga, where else other than in your waters shall I wash my bloodied body?

'Hey, who's that? Aren't you Ratan?'

'Yes, Kaka!'

'Where are you going at this time of the day?'

How could I lie to him? Ram Kaka measured paddy at the weekly market. He was returning home now. Kaka would go past our house and carry on further. Past Shyama's house, and then along the side of the canal towards Maulana Mati's mosque. I told him, 'I'm going to the river jetty.'

Kaka was aghast. 'At this time? Hey, why aren't you saying anything?'

I was silent.

'Hey!'

I stayed silent.

Kaka shook me. 'Tell me the truth. Why are you looking like this?' Ram Kaka then seemed to shudder in shock. 'It looks like blood! Who hurt you?'

How could I stay silent! 'Parimal! He banged my head against a bamboo post. There's a cut. I'm going to the riverbank to wash myself!'

'Which Parimal? The one whose house is on the canal bank? Janardan Saha's son?'

When I lowered my head, he understood. Kaka put his arms around me. 'Come, don't go alone in this darkness, I'll take you there.'

I was captive to Ram Kaka now. 'Why did he hit you? Did you do anything?'

'No. I had plucked and eaten a grapefruit of theirs. Perhaps someone told him about it. That's why he hit me.'

'Eesh, what boys have become!' He continued dejectedly, 'It's an educated household, and yet they're so narrow-minded? Does anyone hurt someone like this?'

'Kaka, please wash off the blood but don't wet my pants.'

'But there's blood on your pants!'

'Let it be, I'll scrape it off with my nails.'

'What'll go wrong if I wet it a little bit? Don't be like this.'

'What if Ma sees my wet pants and wants to know what happened? She'll get alarmed if she hears about it.'

Kaka understood.

The waters of the Nabaganga were still. Ma was right. The river lay down to sleep at this time. It was drowsy before it fell asleep. The narrow bamboo bridge was visible in the distance, next to the Kali temple. The tin-sheet roofs of the small shops in the marketplace were visible too. The shops slanted towards the river. One of those was our shop. Baba's shop. A little booth made of bamboo matting, propped up by bamboo posts, with a flap to shut it. What was Baba doing now? A haircut or a shave? Or was he cleaning the lantern with a rag?

'Come, let me take you home.'

I couldn't protest. The blood would not have been washed off so well if Kaka hadn't been there. The Nabaganga's water level receded in winter. Which was why the road was considerably higher than the jetty. 'Hold my hand.'

'No, Kaka, I can manage by myself.'

Give Me Alms, Ma!

'Will you come somewhere with me?' Ma said to me.

'Where?'

'Will you come or not?'

'I'll come but not in these clothes!'

'Why are you worrying about your clothes now? What's wrong with these?' And as she said that, Ma came up to me. She said, 'Where will we get nice clothes? Are we that fortunate?'

'Why are you talking like that? Does one wear torn clothes when one goes for an outing?'

'You're right, but we aren't really going anywhere. We'll just go for a walk in the hamlet. Or we could go further as well. Let's go now, and then we can decide where to go!'

'Shall I take the rope along? What about the axe?'

'Take them. There isn't a single piece of wood left. Would I be able to carry a load of wood if you weren't there? And we'll have an outing too. Come, let's go while it's still daylight. Where's the small basket?'

'What do we need the basket for?'

'What else ...'

Then I remembered telling Ma, 'Can you make kochu-makha again, Ma? The curry made with taro and large potatoes is really tasty!'

I figured out now why Ma wanted me to take the basket.

'If we find anything lying around while we're gathering twigs, we'll pick it up.'

I laughed. 'But, Ma, I gave you a sack of leaves just a few days ago!'

'How long does your sack of leaves last, my dear? It gets over in a couple of days. How long will it last if we use only leaves for fuel? How many times can I ask you to fetch it—you'll skip school, pick up the sack and run off. But it's your holiday today, that's why! We can gather twigs now so they'll last for many days.'

I thought to myself that we would take the same route we did the other day. Sit at the jetty and gaze at the grasshoppers, the pigs in Bunopara, the piglets suckling. We would sit for a while and then return home. 'So let's go! Which way do you want to go? Towards the jungle?'

'Let's set out first.'

'Let's go. Shall I take the spade along?'

'No. We can't manage so many things.'

It was a quiet afternoon. We didn't go through the hamlet. Ma took the road beside the banyan tree and headed westwards. But no matter where she went, after all I would accompany her.

After going past the banyan tree and crossing the canal, Chhoto Mama's house was a short distance away. Very close to the riverbank. The strip of land between his house and the riverbank also belonged to him. He grew eggplant there. The long thin variety. Each one was almost as long as an arm. A deep purple colour. There was a fine crop of bitter gourd too. And if there were any vacant spots in the field, Mama planted chilli there. And when the plants became robust, red chillies, like sentries, danced on the small plants.

Dada used to go to that field to water the plants. I too used to go, to clear the weeds. Mama's eggplant field meant it was ours too. Dada had once plucked a few eggplants from there. Someone told Mami about that. She got very angry. She went to the field and began hitting Dada. She hit him in the eye by mistake. His right eye swelled up as if he had been stung by a bee. It became bloodshot, and swollen like a potato.

Ma didn't know. As soon as she saw Dada, she began screaming. 'How did that happen? Who did you get into a fight with?' She kept asking him, 'Can you see, Dulal? Can you see me? Oh God, what have you gone and done, my dear!'

After Dada said, 'I can see', she calmed down. And then she asked, 'Who hit you? The corner of your eye is also bruised. How did that happen? Who did you get into a fight with?'

After hearing everything, Ma suddenly turned silent. She didn't say a word. I realised Ma was terribly angry with Mami.

She had held on to that anger ever since. She stopped going to Chhoto Mama's house after that incident. She didn't let us go either. If I ever ran into Mama, I remembered Ma. I walked on with my head lowered. Mama would call out, 'How are you, my boy? Why don't you visit?'

I didn't go to Mama's house, but how could I avoid that road if I wanted to head westwards? The road we were on went past Mama's house. It wasn't as if there was no other way. One could go down the embankment and walk along the river. Then walk along the bank to the other jetty. And if one climbed up the embankment from there, it was possible to avoid Mama's house altogether. Is that what Ma would do?

Ma had asked me to take along a rope. I had done that. It would be needed to tie together the twigs. The rope was in the basket. Ma placed a hand on my shoulder. I was walking slowly. With measured steps. 'Do you have only one pair of pants?'

I looked at Ma. The drawstring of my pants was hanging till my knees. As soon as she noticed that, she tucked it into my waist. 'I wear the other one to school.'

Ma laughed. She knew everything, but she still asked. Did she want to annoy me? Was she testing me, to see what I would say when I got annoyed? Is that why she asked?

'Why do you ask me?'

'The cloth's faded. It's torn in two places.'

I felt bad. 'I thought you were taking me for an outing, and then I realised that we're going to collect twigs. So I wore the right thing, didn't I?'

Ma too said, 'I was right too.'

'Yes'. Both of us laughed.

She looked at me again with kindly eyes. 'Don't be sad, dear! People live in great difficulty. We're in the same plight! You'll earn when you grow up, and then you'll have all the clothes you need.'

Ma held me close. I buried my face in her waist. I walked like that. That smell. I loved it! Ma had the kind of sweet smell which was there on the quilt and mattress when one put them out in the hot sun. An old smell, but it seemed new. It was this smell that made me fall asleep every night.

After we advanced some more, it was as I had thought. Ma said we would go down to the riverside. 'Hold me. Walk down slowly.'

'You don't have to hold me! I can jump down, you know! You go down, I'll manage on my own.'

The riverbank was covered in reeds. As I hurried down the slope, a group of bank-mynahs flew off from a hole, *kilik*. A mongoose sped away and stopped and stood still at a distance. It looked at us with alert eyes. As if to see what we were doing, where we were going. Or did the mongoose think that we wanted to kill it? 'Come,' said Ma.

We were at the riverside. Ma was holding my hand. The river took a turn just ahead. An acacia branch lay on the bank at the turn, lapped by the water. 'Isn't that a fish-catching egret, Ma?'

'Where?'

'There, where the acacia branch is lying. Can you see it?'

'Yes, I can! It's resting. But it's alert.'

We walked along the bank. 'Wait, Ratan. My sari's got caught on something,' Ma said.

'Hang on, I'll free it.' I bent down to free her sari from a dry piece of wood. I said, 'It's almost done. The Majumdar household's jetty is nearby.'

'You seem to know everything!'

'Why wouldn't I know it? I used to go to Mama's house, didn't I?'

I wanted to ask her whether Mami would get angry if we went along the road. After all, the road belonged to the government.

'Hurry up, we have to return home before it gets dark.'

I rarely came to these parts. We usually headed towards the town and the marketplace—we hardly ever went in the opposite direction.

The marketplace. Nandol School. The cinema hall. Bhaynar Mor. The dam built by WAPDA. Nomani Maidan. All these places were towards the town. But we were walking in the opposite direction today. From where people took the road that went past the banyan tree near our house. Here, the more we advanced, the more rural it became. A remote village. Full of greenery. Flocks of birds. Ma knew all these wooded parts well. If we looked around, we would surely find pieces of wood lying around, which was what we had come for.

This was the Baidya household of Batkedanga. They had a lychee orchard. Past that was an areca grove. The house of the Baidyas was surrounded by these. There were many rooms there. The Durga Pujo here was a grand affair. A goat was sacrificed. The *dhakis*, or drummers, performed dances with ankle-bells on their feet. *Dadda natang*! The boys from this house taunted me if I encountered them during the Durga Pujo. 'Didn't you feed your *asur*? Just go and see ours!' Ma and I were going past that house.

There was a tile-roofed hut near the areca grove. It had a waist-high fence all around it. The flowers on the creepers growing on it stretched out their necks. A man sitting on his haunches suddenly stood up. He looked very familiar! Wasn't it that sadhu? Wasn't he the one who used to come to our village to beg for alms with his blind son? It was indeed that sadhu! 'Gour Haribol! Ma, will you give me some alms?'

Yes, it was him. He never got anything from our house. But he still came. As if he thought, even if they didn't give me anything today, they might tomorrow. Or was that the rule when they came to a hamlet to beg. Ma didn't ask him to go away. She didn't like him leaving empty-handed. I used to go and tell him, 'Excuse us!' On some days I lied, saying, 'There's no one at home!' He would then leave.

I would observe the boy's eyes while speaking to his father. There were only sockets instead of eyes. No eyelids, no eyeballs. He held his father's hand. He nodded his head. There was a *tilak* on his forehead. It looked nice. When I said, 'excuse us', that meant telling the same to him too. He would go to another house, holding his father's hand and nodding his head. You were not supposed to get angry when you were asked to leave. Some people gave something, while others didn't. Like we did not.

Why did their departure make me feel so sad? Perhaps the boy would have been in Class III like me if he had eyesight. I kept gazing at them. At the boy holding his father's hand. Two people leaving our house. It was I who had sent them away. Without a fistful of rice.

We really had no rice to give as alms. That's why we sent them away.

Perhaps Ma could return the rice she had borrowed if fistfuls of rice were saved in this way. She did that too. She used to keep aside three fistfuls of rice with her left hand. And in winter like now, that was used. It was Ma who said, 'I have a longstanding debt of rice and potatoes to people in the hamlet. I'm unable to return anything to anyone. I'm too ashamed to go out.'

Achchha, could one sleep if one didn't have eyeballs?

Seeing the man face to face, I felt ashamed. He was of Baba's age, but I addressed him with the disrespectful 'tumi' because he was a beggar. As we went past the hut, the image of the man standing in our courtyard floated before my eyes. 'Give me some alms, Ma!' Was the boy inside the hut? Had his father kept him inside because he couldn't see?

I imagined the beggar boy with the tilak on his forehead lying down. He would surely have recognised me if he had heard my voice. He too would have remembered the 'excuse us'. He would know it was me who was going past their hut. But I no longer felt bad; after all, we were poor too. We too had come to forage fuelwood in order to be able to cook. Foraging meant picking up something that was lying around, not asking anyone for anything. But this too was an unstated form of begging.

Heeding Ma, I too took a different route, not the one with houses. That would have been easy and quick too. After all, it was I who went to all the houses with a plate. 'Khurima, Ma asked for a little bit of rice. She'll return it on the market day.' Some households gave it, while some didn't. I felt even more ashamed to mention Ma's name.

Hardly anyone came to the shop for haircuts because it was the winter season. This was a time of penury. The rainy season too was like that. The few customers who did come for shaves—how much did that pay? An anna for a shave, while a haircut was two annas. Baba gave them a haircut even if they bargained and reduced the price. It was better to give a customer a haircut than to turn him away. Rice was ten annas a seer. It was the time of Ayub Khan's reign, meaning 1963. Baba quarrelled with Ma almost every day after returning home from the shop. 'How can a single person's earnings fill the bellies of the ogres you've birthed?'

Ma would be silent. Why only Ma, I too understood that there was no money. Baba quarrelled with Ma like this when there was no money.

Baba quarrelled a lot that day. The next morning, again the soft voice, 'Gour Haribol. Please give me some alms, Ma!'

I was unable to say anything when I went outside. The sadhu stood waiting outside for a long time. In case Ma came out and gave him a fistful of alms. After some time, it was the boy who softly said, 'Let's go, Baba, they aren't giving anything.'

That sight. I thought I should tell Ma. It had been on my mind for quite a few days. I always listened to Ma. So wouldn't she listen to me now? Just the other day she was speaking about our Mama-bari. About her childhood. About a swing on the tamarind tree. Gorging on starfruits and wood apples. Raw sour-sweet mangoes were supposed to be plucked using a shell. The class Ma had studied till was also part of this tale. What if I told her, 'Will you go somewhere with me, Ma?'

'Where?'

'Tell me, will you go?'

'I will, but where to?'

'We'll go across the bamboo bridge at Nandol, and then a little beyond Aattharokhoda. Towards the remote village.'

'Why do you need to go there?'

'Be patient, I'll tell you. But you'll go, won't you?'

Hearing that made her thoughtful. 'Tell me what?' Ma knew it wasn't something straightforward. 'Out with it!'

'Enter the courtyard of the house in that village, and just say, "O Ma, Mistress!" I'll be holding your hand.'

Ma gaped at me. Why was she looking at me like that?

'Are you asking me to beg?'

I didn't say a word. Ma was no longer looking at me! Was she angry? Weren't those tears? Had I made Ma cry?

I walked ahead. When the wood was gathered, Ma would tie the bundle and carry the larger branches on her shoulder. I would carry the twigs. She would lift the bundle of twigs up to a coil of cloth on my head. If the load was placed correctly, I would be able to carry it alright.

How much further after Batkedanga? Which wood were we going to?

Baba Left After He Was Done Beating Me

Ma said quite dejectedly, 'Don't take my blessings, pay obeisance at the tulsi pedestal, and go to the Kali temple as well.'

I looked back. Ma wasn't there. I was going for an examination, but for some reason I didn't feel like going. Would Ma continue to be unhappy? I would have gone even if Ma hadn't told me. After all it was Ma who reminded me to offer namaskar at the Kali temple. And not just before exams; if I was going somewhere far away, or even going to the marketplace, offering pranam at the Kali temple was like a rule. Just as I took leave of Ma while setting out from home, I did the same at the Kali temple.

Ma didn't peep out. Perhaps she went inside as soon as she said that. Yes, I would go. I had gone at the time of the half-yearly exams as well. After offering pranam, I shut my eyes and inwardly touched Ma Kali's feet. And then I muttered, 'Dear Ma, let me do well, if I pass I'll make an offering of five-and-a-quarter annas of *batasha*.' I made the same vow at the tulsi pedestal. The Kali temple was right opposite our shop. Ashu Thakur was the priest there. He rang the bell there, *dong!*

As soon as I left home, I took the path going towards the school. I offered pranam at the Kali temple. I made the vow about passing the exam. But why hadn't Ma accepted my pranam? Why did she say, 'Don't take my blessings? Pay obeisance to the tulsi plant, go to the Kali temple as well?' Why did she say this? Was it because she was feeling unhappy? I felt a sense of unease as I came out of the Kali temple.

There they were. Everyone was on their way to the exam today. I encountered some of my friends from the neighbourhood too. I think they went to the temple too. But they didn't speak to me. They taunted me through insinuations. What had they pledged? More than me? They would surely pledge more than five-and-a-quarter annas.

They were looking at me again and again. I walked quickly. But Swapan still said out loud, 'How much can it be! How can the barber afford more than an anna!'

Yes, he was referring to the vow. Let him say whatever he wanted to. I paid no heed. As if I hadn't heard them. I didn't want to hear either. If Ma Kali passed me for the offering of five-and-a-quarter annas, I would make it, or else I would have to repeat the class. There was no need to offer more. I couldn't afford that either.

But after making my plea to God, I got worried. Five-and-a-quarter annas in two places. Adding up, that was ten-and-a-half annas. I would have to arrange for the money as soon as the exam got over. The results would be out in a few days. I would make the offering even if I passed 'on consideration'. I had said to Ma Kali, 'I'll make an offering if I do well.' But since I had made a vow, I would definitely buy the batasha even if I didn't do well but merely passed. I would also make an offering to Hari at the tulsi pedestal at home. I would buy the batasha and then go first to the Kali temple, and then come home. When one made a vow to God for something, one had to keep it. God apparently kept it in mind if one didn't do that.

One was not supposed to tell anyone about a vow. I wouldn't either. Only God knew, and I. Let them offer more, they were wealthy folk, they could afford it. I would not be able to keep up with them when it came to making vows.

The fish market was just ahead, past Haripada Kaka's tea shop. Going past that, I arrived near the bamboo bridge. I guessed the others weren't far behind. My eyes suddenly turned to the jute warehouse. I imagined a large bunch of areca pods. Of raw areca. That's it! No more worry! It was this areca that would save me. There was no need to be worried about ten-and-a-half annas!

Where was the need for worry when I could pluck the areca from some households? A sickle tucked at my waist. But no, we didn't have a sickle. We had an axe though. The one with which I went to fetch firewood. That would suffice. I didn't need anything else. There were many areca groves near Maulana Mati's house. I would go to those houses. 'Shall I pluck your areca, Sir?'

It was customary to pay four areca nuts if one plucked the areca from a tree. Even if someone reduced that by one because I was small, I would do the plucking. The way Baba didn't let customers go, and gave them shaves and haircuts for less, I too wouldn't let a tree go. If I didn't, someone else would pluck it. I needed the money desperately. I had to have the money ready before the results were out—by any means whatsoever.

Without paying heed to anyone, and without looking at anything, I went up to the bamboo bridge. Our school was on the other side. I pranced to make the bridge sway. I felt excited after seeing the areca tree. As if I wanted to go at once to all those houses and tell the folks, 'Get me to pluck your areca, Chacha! If you have lots of trees, I'll do it for less!'

'Let them ripen a bit. Will you climb the tree?'

'I can do it. I'm skinny. I do it all the time. I pluck areca at so many households. Shall I climb up?'

'No. But I can see that you can do it.'

I imagined all that, I heard it all.

It really wouldn't be difficult at all to climb up the areca tree. I'd race up, however tall it was. And then I just had to take it to the wholesale section of the weekly market. I was so happy that the lines of a poem in my textbook seemed to float in front of my eyes. Lines of prose as well.

Soon after crossing the bridge, as I turned at the booth of the toll collector, I saw that all the students had come empty-handed. But I had brought my books and slate. Was one not supposed to bring one's books at exam time? Had I done that in Class II? I couldn't remember.

The boys from the neighbourhood were very studious. Was I like that? Of course not. I heard the hum of their memorisation as I sat at home. I used to memorise mentally. But that enraged Baba. He thought one had to say it aloud. So that not just the folks at home, but people outside too understood that someone was studying in the house. That's what Baba wanted. Chhor-da had given up his studies. No one in our family had completed school and passed the Matric examination. All my dadas had left midway. When they were in Class V or VI. But Baba wanted me to be a Matriculate. I would be the first in my family to do that. But as Baba saw it, that would happen only if I said my lessons out loud.

One day Baba asked me, 'What are you looking at with the book on your lap?' After that he exclaimed, 'Is this how you're studying?' And at once, he landed a blow. Baba left after he was done beating me.

'What are you doing? Do you want to kill the boy?' Ma wailed.

'Let him die! Let the house be emptied one by one!'

Ma too added to that, 'Why should I be left out?'

'You won't be left out either after this!'

Ma then came and massaged my back. She pressed her anchal down on the painful spots. I placed my head on Ma's lap and sobbed.

After that day, I recited my lessons out loud. So loud, that the voice of anyone else studying in the hamlet was drowned out. But not at all times. I did that only so long as Baba was at home. Why was Baba angry all the time?

To tell the truth, I didn't like to study. Chhor-da had discontinued his studies, and he didn't want to do anything else. But if anyone said anything to him, he gave back an earful. Baba told him, 'Go wherever you like. See for yourself how joyful living outside is!'

'I'll go when it's time. You don't need to tell me.'

Ma became alarmed. Me too. Would Chhor-da go away? And never return? Not even to visit? I didn't ever say such things. Sometimes, after a thrashing, I too felt like saying something like Chhor-da did. But no. I checked myself. After all it was Baba. Could one talk back to him?

Baba had no clue that I did so many things with Ma. Did anyone ever talk about their personal matters? Fetching fuelwood. Borrowing rice. Plucking spinach and greens. If I used a fishing rod and caught a fish, it was Baba who exclaimed, 'Did Ratan catch such a big shol fish?'

I did all of that. And studied too in the midst of it. Did my friends in the hamlet also have to do all this? But I was very worried today. If the vow to God involved more money, which side would God favour? Would Ma Kali give them better results than me?

'Hey you idiot, does anyone come with books on exam day?' Subol Sir was standing in front of the classroom door. 'Go and keep them in the staff room. Come back quickly.'

Thank God the boys weren't nearby now. Who knows what they would have said if they were present. But perhaps they wouldn't say too much because it was exam day. I kept my books, and just as I was about to go past Sir, he said, 'Didn't you take a bath? Your hair is all dishevelled!'

I kept quiet. I thought I would go into the classroom without saying anything to Sir. Or should I tell him that Baba beat me very badly yesterday? He quarrelled a lot with Ma too. Apparently, she was going to leave for Boro Mama's house. Baba had said, 'Begone all of you!' No food was cooked today, Sir! I didn't have a bath either.

I hadn't thought about all that. It was Sir who brought it to mind. It didn't linger on my mind either. I only saw the kitchen shut when there was quarrelling going on inside. I would leave the house and walk towards the nearby houses. Maybe someone would call me. Maybe they would give me a bit to eat before getting me to do some work.

I found Ma lying down whenever I returned home. She didn't seem to care when I returned or what I ate. I hovered around her. Was Ma very sick? She used to say a lot of things earlier while quarrelling. But since that made Baba even angrier, she just listened to him quietly nowadays. I used to gaze at the two of them at such times. Would Baba hit her? If he made to hit Ma, I would stop him. But no, that never happened. Only a verbal fight. But for some reason, I now thought Baba would hit Ma one day.

'Go in!' Sir said.

He saw so many boys. Heard so much talk. Talk about home. About illness, not having books, the house being destroyed in the storm, the pillars not being replaced yet. Sir listened attentively to all such talk. He knew that most of the students were from poor households. That's why Subol Sir wanted to hear about various things, and not just about classroom matters.

He listened to us and said nice things. He said, 'You must study and put an end to their difficulties.' Perhaps Sir understood why I hadn't had a bath. Although he didn't know that there had been no cooking because of a quarrel, nevertheless it seemed like he sensed something was amiss.

Moulovi Sir had distributed the question papers in our class a little while ago.

Will You Go Away, My Dear?

I was under the banyan tree again. The boys played football every day after the exams were over. Ashit and I used to play with grapefruits. Play meaning, he would kick a grapefruit towards me. And then I would kick it back. He didn't tell me whose tree the grapefruit had been pilfered from. When I asked him, he retorted, 'Why do you need to know? You're playing, so keep playing!'

'It would have ripened in a few days!'

'Sure it would! Kick it now!'

I kicked it with all my strength. And the moment I did that, I cried out, 'Ooh! I hurt myself! Is it Parimal's grapefruit?'

There was a smile on Ashit's face. His legs were stronger than mine. And sturdier. While I was scrawny. I was just not putting on weight. Perhaps I wouldn't be so skinny if I ate a bit more rice. Ashit's family were poor too. Not as poor as us, but poor nonetheless. Kaka's shop was beside the weekly vegetable market. After he was done with his selling when the market closed, he paid off the rice wholesaler. He did not have a shop anywhere else. The weekly market was held two days a week. While my Baba's shop was open every day. Whether he gave people haircuts or shaves, it all added up, and yet we were so needy.

A rice shop meant there was rice that could be eaten. If only Baba had a shop like that, we wouldn't be short of food. If only the price of haircuts rose. No, no one in the village would pay any more. As it is, I had observed people coming for a haircut and then haggling over the price. Baba's face seemed to shrink at that. He couldn't say what was on his mind. Yet he would ask, 'You've come with a whole month's beard, is an anna too much?' Perhaps in Ashit's household they got their fill of rice. That's why he was healthy. His feet were tough. He was stronger too. My legs began to ache after a few kicks. I thought I had sprained my ankle. But how could I declare 'I won't play' so soon?

Ashit was observant. 'Hey, it looks like you're limping! You princeling! Here, kick! Kick it hard! Do you eat sago at home or what!'

'No, I won't play. Let's play something else.' I was limping towards him. 'Hey, will you help me a bit?'

Ashit was alarmed. He supported me with his shoulder, and sat me down gently. The moment he touched my feet, I screamed out, 'O Ma!'

'Hang on!' Ashit growled. He placed his palm on the bone and massaged it. He seemed to be muttering something under his breath. Was it a mantra?

'You know a mantra? What is it? Say it a bit louder!'

'I just made up some nonsense!' And he burst out laughing.

'Why are you laughing?'

Actually he had uttered a word at the end. A bad word. A swear word. We knew such things. 'Don't joke around! Take me home.'

Ma wouldn't get scared today. There was no bleeding, but she would know as soon as she saw me that I had hurt myself while playing. I knew that it was Ma who would now apply lime and turmeric on the spot. I hadn't told her about Parimal having beaten me up the last time. I had turned my head in another direction before encountering Ma. She had asked me, 'Why haven't you bathed for the last few days?'

That was when I told her, 'I didn't tell you that I grazed my head a bit on a branch while climbing a tree.'

I had concealed the wound on my head. But I felt lighter after telling her. Ma wanted to take a look. I had covered up the cut with my hair, so she wouldn't notice it. If my foot swelled up today, it was Ma who would take care of it. She would know what to do. We were headed homewards now. 'You're so light!'

Ashit, who was the same age as me, was almost carrying me. From the banyan tree to our house, past six houses. Dry bark from the areca tree had been strung from the bamboo roof trusses all around our house. Baba had done that so no one could see inside, since the house was beside the road. My job was to fetch dry bark wherever I spotted any. I had to discard the bark that had rotted after a few days of rain and replace them with new ones.

My arm was around Ashit's neck and I was leaning on his shoulder. We reached my house. Should I enter right now? 'Khurima, come here quickly!'

Was Ma awaiting the call? Perhaps mothers sensed bad news. She came out in such a hurry that she just missed knocking down the areca barrier by a bit. 'What's happened Ashit? What is it? Why aren't you saying anything?'

'Nothing serious. We were playing around with a grapefruit and he hurt his foot a bit. It's nothing like what Ratan is making it out to be, Khurima!' Ashit then looked at me and said, 'Hey, stand up, nothing's happened to you! It'll be fine after applying hot turmeric for two days. Isn't it, Khurima?'

Ma was a bit calm now. 'Where's the need to go to play? Is he strong at all? You're bound to hurt yourself like this if you go to play with this jute-stalk figure of yours. Serves you right! Lie in bed for a couple of days now!'

'Hey Khurima, there's no need for that!' Ashit said, with a wise air. He said, 'Ratan's become tough after all the beating. I always see him returning from a beating! And this was just a small injury on his foot.'

But Ma seemed not to be listening to all that. 'Straighten your leg.' Ma placed my foot on the ground and asked me, 'Can you stand on this?'

'Ooh! It hurts!'

Ashit stood beside me with a worried look. After all, he was the one who had called me out to play. Perhaps he was feeling bad. How on earth did I get hurt? Yes, now I could recall that I had hurt myself while trying to kick the fruit hard. I was listening to Ma now. I would have to listen to her silently even if she scolded me. Through the pain, I said to Ashit, 'Hey Ashit, why are you standing? Sit down.'

'Do you have turmeric, Khurima? Or shall I bring some from home? Heat and apply it, all the pain will go away.'

'Do that. Open the latch on our kitchen door, and you'll see the turmeric container on the half-wall on the side. Bring it, and I'll do it.'

Ashit ran in, and returned with the container. Ma said, 'See if there's a broken tin in the corner of the veranda. If it's there, we can use that to heat the turmeric. Just do that please. I'll take care of the rest.'

Ashit left. There he was, going through the grassy undergrowth. He was the first of my peers from the village who began working. He had come to our house after a long time. He would leave again. He was a helper on the motor bus. He said that after being a helper, he would become a conductor, and then as soon as he learnt to drive, he would become a driver. A driver's salary was significant. Let some time go by, and then I would ask Ashit, 'Will you take me along?'

It wasn't only Ashit, almost everyone attended school for a couple of years or so and then left. They began by selling the greens and fruits grown at home, and then turned into shopkeepers one day. Chhor-da too had left school. Ashit dropped out somewhat early as well. If only I could have got a job in Jessore like him. He looked in better health because he was away from home. He had an amulet around his neck. Was that so he would grow strong? The amulet seemed to wiggle when he spoke. He was happy with his job in Jessore.

The motor bus was like a dream for me. The metalled road. New villages. The conductor standing at the door. Hair blowing in the wind. When one was on a bus, the trees beside seemed to be running backwards. And if one looked further into the distance, one saw the boundary ridges winding through the fields. What was Ashit's job on the bus? What did a helper do?

I went to his house the next day. He was startled to see me. 'You've come despite the injury.'

'What can I do, how can one just sit at home all day? What are you doing?'

'I'll pack my clothes in a little while. My Ma's made a package with *chira*, *moa* and *patali*. I'm off at dawn tomorrow.'

'Will you look for a job for me, Ashit?'

'Why do you want to go? Didn't you just take the exam? How will you work if you are promoted to the next class? Will Khurima allow you to go?'

'Why wouldn't she? Let me tell you, Ma herself will want me to go.'

'Will you really go?' Ashit seemed to be perplexed. 'I'll tell my employer. He has many buses. I'll tell him that you're my village friend. Give him a job too!'

It seemed certain that he would take me along when he came home next. Where would Ma go to forage fuelwood once I left? Would she be able to venture far all by herself? Would Chhor-da do all that once I left? Didn't Baba say that he couldn't carry on feeding ogres. I think Baba too would be in favour of my leaving. If all of us found some kind of job, what more could Baba ask for?

I put my arm around Ashit's shoulder. 'I'll go!'

Ma gave me an earful the moment I returned home. 'Why did you go out with this swollen foot?'

I had walked using my foot smeared in yellow. I felt a stinging pain now. I realised Ma was terribly angry with me. But I still went and sat close to her, and said, 'Don't worry about me.'

But it seemed like Ma didn't hear that. I then said, 'Shall I tell you something?'

Ma looked at me. Why was she breathless? 'Are you feeling unwell?'

'What's that to you?'

'I was saying … what if I went to work like Ashit?'

'Where?'

'Where he works, in Jessore. Working as a helper on a bus. Once one learns the job, one becomes a conductor. And after doing that for a while, once I learn to drive, I'll get a good salary.'

'Will you go away, my dear! Won't you continue your studies?'

Our Results Come Out Today

The school was reopening today after a long break. The exam results would be declared too. There seemed to be a stillness all through the hamlet. Someone or the other had taken the exams in almost every household. Ma didn't know. I was the one who told her about the results. She listened to me. But she didn't say anything. She was lying down a lot nowadays. Ma had become ill all of a sudden. We used to do so much work together even until a few days ago. So many tasks. She didn't talk about work anymore. Baba did the household chores before he left. It remained undone if he couldn't. All Baba was concerned about was his shop. He could not worry about whether or not there was someone at home, or whether they were dying. He opened the shop in the morning. If it was opened before the other shops then it was our shop that customers would enter. Even if there was a single early customer, that meant more money.

It was for this money that Ma too sent me to the shop. Especially when I didn't go to school. Baba made me sit in front of the shop. He asked me to ensure that no one went away. Very often, customers came to ask for work to be done at their home. That work could be in a household where a baby had been born. The mother's nails and the baby's tiny nails had to be ritually touched with the chisel-like nail cutter called *norun* before they left the confines of the *aantur*, or labour room, which was considered impure. One did not have to be an adult to do that. Actually they preferred a boy like me. If it was an adult, the new mother would have to draw her ghomta over her head.

The haircutting salon next to ours belonged to Debu Kaka. He had three daughters. Girls were not supposed to use the nail cutter. It was good for Baba that I was a boy. He sent me when such jobs came up. Wrapping the nail cutter in paper, Baba would tell me, 'Cut the nails very carefully.'

I walked to faraway villages accompanied by the people of the household where the job needed to be done. Sometimes my legs ached as I walked all that distance. But I still went. While walking I imagined the courtyard of the house. Chira, *murki* and curd served on a banana leaf. The *bhujyi*, or ritual offering to the barber of rice heaped in a clay pot. A pair of betel leaves with areca. A rupee coin. I would offer a namaskar from afar to the mother with a baby at her bosom. I felt terribly embarrassed then. Does one do namaskar to an infant? Apparently one was supposed to do that. I would mix the curd with the chira and murki. It was usually the womenfolk who stood nearby. They said, 'Eat to your fill.'

I ate too. Hearing their exhortations from close proximity made one think that not everyone beat up poor folk, some were affectionate too. Aah! How long it had been since I had eaten so well. The people of the household made a bundle of the things I was supposed to receive, so that I wouldn't have to do that with my small hands. 'Are you sure you'll be able to make your way back?'

'Yes.' And I would return all by myself carrying the bhujyi.

As soon as I reached the shop, Baba would ask me, 'What did they give you to eat?' I had eaten a bellyful. I would say, 'Such a lot of murki! How sweet the curd was!'

'Didn't they give you any fruits?'

'No.'

'Each house has its own customs. These people don't, that's why they didn't. Was the clay pot heaped with rice?'

'Yes, Baba, I was watching, it was heaped. A pair of betel leaves on top of that, with two areca nuts in the middle.'

'So the pot was heaped. Some people just hand you the rice in a bag ... didn't they give you anything else?'

Baba had fond hopes. 'No, Baba.'

'Anyway, it's over and done with in the morning. That's good.' And as he said that, he turned the rupee coin and looked at both sides. After that he put it into the pocket of his *fotua*.

I sat in front of the shop. The road to the school lay ahead. If some who knew me walked by, they asked, 'What's up, Ratan, aren't you going to school?'

I looked at them blankly, as if I hadn't heard them. Not receiving a reply, they went away. And then when I realised after some time that it was past the time for the school bell to ring, *Dong!* I could tell who was sitting where even without being in school. I would be right at the back. I didn't want to sit on the front bench either. I was taunted. That didn't happen if I sat on the last bench. In fact, sitting at the back meant having come to school without doing the homework, hence being punished for that. So it was the last-benchers that Sir hauled up. 'Hey, stand up!'

It was only after going over my lessons that I went to school. When I missed school, I memorised the next lesson. Why should I tell anyone why I hadn't come yesterday? I didn't mind sitting on the last bench. But I had to learn the lesson because Sir asked the last benchers to say it aloud.

I didn't go to the shop. I hadn't gone for quite a few days. Besides, it was the day of the exam results. Baba didn't say anything. He was busy quarrelling with Ma nowadays. He was hitting me too. Chhor-da watched me getting beaten. There was nothing he could do other than watch. If he confronted Baba's anger, he would get beaten too. Baba had hidden a stick-like branch in the bamboo roof truss. I found the stick there one day when Baba was away at the shop. And as I gazed at it, I ran my fingers over the swollen welts on my arm from the beating. Would Ma take me along if she went away to her father's house? But how would she go there? It was far away.

It seemed like any other day. But all those I encountered on the way to school were strangely silent. Robi, Swapan, Dipu and I were all beside one another. We were walking but no one made a casteist slur today!

Had they gone to the Kali temple? Ma was unwell; she hadn't seen me off. I knew I would break into tears the moment I stood before Ma Kali, and so I hadn't gone. If I passed, I would first run with the results and show it to Ma, 'I've passed, see my results!' And after that to Ma Kali. Had I done anything wrong by not going to the Kali temple before coming to school? All kinds of thoughts flooded my mind. Why did the boys behave like that with me?

What was my fault? I couldn't understand it. Did beating me, and not letting me enter their houses make them very happy? I didn't mind it so much when they didn't let me join their games, but they always referred to my caste. I know they did that because we had nothing. But it pained me very much when they had fun at my expense like that. *Achchha*, the school that Ma went to, the one in Ramdebganti, was that still there? It suddenly occurred to me, what if Ma took me there and admitted me to that school? I would continue my education living in my Mama-bari. Couldn't I get admitted there? And then I thought, what if they said I would need to bring documents from Magura because I was from elsewhere. What would I do then? Did we have any documents?

I would fall at their feet and say, 'My Ma was a student of your school.' Wouldn't they believe me? They might, but they might not too. If they did, perhaps they would admit me. I would remain there then. But if Ashit found me a job before that, I wouldn't take admission at that school. After all, education was for getting a job. If I found one at an early age, what was wrong with that? Ashit would surely ask around on my behalf. He wouldn't lie to me.

I couldn't figure out what I ought to do. Ma's illness, Baba's quarrelling, me getting beaten. I was very worried. Would Ashit be able to find me a job? I would stay in my Mama's house until then and continue my studies. I didn't like this village any longer. If only Ashit had sent a message through someone—Ratan, come over! Get into a bus going to Jessore at Bhayna in Magura, and say, 'Jessore bus stand'. Tell the conductor my name. If you do that, he might let you travel without paying the fare. Say you are Ashit's friend. A lot of people know me.

Say that you're going in order to work on a bus. *Oof*, why didn't everything happen right away? So that as soon as I got down at the destination, I would be a conductor on the very next bus itself, calling out, 'Jhineda, Jhineda, Gopalpur!'

Satish Sir said, 'It's the day of your results today. I am reading out the names of the first ten students. After that the names of those who have passed in all subjects, and then those passed on consideration. I won't say any more after that. Those who have failed should go home and start studying the books of this class again. The one who has come first is Kalpana Chakraborty, second is Ratan Biswas, third ...'

Why wasn't I feeling happy? Why did I not feel like running home? As I climbed on to the narrow wooden bridge, I looked in the direction of the areca tree. I could fulfil my pledge at any later point in time. Of course, that didn't mean after many years. Let the rainy season arrive, I would be able to save money from the regular garden work then. And plucking the areca was there of course.

I wouldn't make the offering to Hari at our tulsi pedestal right now. I know no one would come for the offering ceremony if I invited them. I wasn't worried about that either. It would be just Ma, Bhombol, and me. I wouldn't exclude Bhombol just because he was a dog. Ma had told me that one should love every creature. And after all, Bhombol was one of us. No matter where he was, he would come as soon as he was called. I would buy five-and-a-quarter annas worth of batasha and go to the tulsi pedestal. 'Hari Hari Bol' would be chanted, and the offering made in a saucer. It was Ma who did the prayers, so she would make the offering to God by chanting his name, and then give it to us. To

Bhombol and me. That was it, no one else was needed. How would it matter if I didn't call anyone else?

I stood in front of the shop. Baba was asleep. With his right leg lifted up to a corner of the bench. His hands were tucked into his chest. His head resting against the wall of bamboo lath matting. The weight of his head made a dent in the matting. Was Baba snoring? There, *ghor-ghor!* It was only once I was inside the shop that I opened my results sheet. Progress Report. There was a '19' printed on one side, and beside that '63' written with ink. Meaning the year 1963. There was a long blank line below that. Sir had written there: 'Nanduyali Free Primary School'. Below that was my name. And on the upper right side, 'Second', written in red ink. I would have shown Baba the green-coloured report card, but I had never seen him so soundly asleep before. Let him sleep, I thought.

As I went past the paan yard near Beltala, I felt a stinging pain. And before I knew anything—what's this? Who threw a stone at me!

I stopped. No, there was no ripe wood apple. Had a jungle cat leapt on me? After pausing awhile, I continued walking. And suddenly, once again! 'O Ma-a-a!' Although I lay twisted on the earth, I spotted the stone that had hit me on my back, it was lying near me. I looked behind me. No, there wasn't anyone there. I got up and began running. And as I ran, I called out, 'O Ma!'

I ran even faster. The banyan tree was ahead. A few more houses. Perhaps I wouldn't be able to make it. I was panting. My throat was dry. I felt like something was stuck inside my chest. I again called out full-throatedly. 'O Ma, come quickly! They're going to kill me … Ma!'

Ratan's Got Scabies!

Why on earth was I assailed by scabies as soon as winter arrived? Was it an ailment? But didn't an ailment mean fever? And becoming thinner by the day, and one's feet swelling up, like the constantly-sleepy Ma? But I had none of that when I got scabies. My entire body itched. It itched so much that I angrily scratched my whole body using my two hands. That provided relief. I basked in the morning sun. A pale liquid oozed out of the scratched body. And a little bit of blood. The sun's heat felt sweet. But after a while, it felt too hot. I would go inside, and call out restlessly, 'O Ma, can you come here for a bit?'

Ma knew everything. She said, 'What do you want me to do?' and ran her hand over my body, exclaiming *'Eesh, eesh'* all the while.

Ma applied raw turmeric and then bathed me in water that had been boiled with neem leaves. She said, 'Bring a few neem branches, I'll tear off the leaves and boil them, and you can bathe in that again.' That would help mitigate the scabies. It needed to be done every day but that didn't happen. Ma wasn't able to do it.

I was to blame too. Breaking off a neem branch was an easy matter, but I didn't do it. The scabies would worsen. And that was painful. So painful that I couldn't go to school. Scabies led to sores oozing with pus. It stank. But one couldn't discern one's own smell.

My friends understood from seeing me walk. I moved with my legs held apart and my pant-legs pulled in front. They saw me entering the classroom like that. They complained to Sir. 'Ratan's got scabies, Sir! He smells. We can't sit near him, Sir!'

Sir asked me to stand up. 'Go home at once! Don't come to school until your scabies has healed.'

I felt ashamed to get up and leave. Even more so because there were several girls in our class. They giggled when Sir asked me to leave.

I got it again this year. I had been feeling very itchy for the last few days. Ma used to apply turmeric on me, and bathe me in neem water. But now? It wasn't that Ma wasn't doing any work. I know she found it difficult. And I couldn't really do anything. I just hovered around her. Ma said, 'Go away, your Ma isn't dying!'

I hoped that was true. It was said that when mothers cursed their children, that didn't come true. Did whatever mothers utter in grief come true? Or was it the opposite? I didn't ask about that, but a lot of nonsense got into my head at various times. But why was I thinking about terrible things? Was Ma's illness the only thing? Or was she not telling the truth because we would feel bad? Was it something like that? When did all this happen? After all, I was always with her. I tried to recall the instances when I had gone out leaving Ma all alone. Had something happened then?

I couldn't figure out anything. Had Baba hit her?

Aah! Why did I think so? I was shocked. I cancelled the thought. No, I hadn't thought that. I didn't! My eyes brimmed with tears. I wiped my eyes. And as I wept, I said to myself, 'I won't think such things! God, take away these thoughts!'

I wasn't bothered about the scabies now. All I could think of was that Ma should get well. I wouldn't let Ma do anything when she was unwell. Let Ma be as she was. Let her do as she pleases. I'll handle everything, Ma!

I would be able to cook rice if I observed her do that for a couple of days. Cooking dal was easy. Two fistfuls of the pink-coloured dal had to be left to boil in a hand's width of water. When it boiled and produced a whitish foam, that meant it was done. Once one twirled the wooden churner on that, it became smooth. After that, it had to be poured into the earthen basin, and a wok had to be heated with four or five drops of oil, and three or four green chillies. That had to be stirred with a ladle, and as soon as the chillies began getting roasted, the basin had to be lifted up using rags and the boiled dal poured into the wok for tempering. Wouldn't I be able to do that?

I would call Ma first. I would say, 'You sit down, I'll bring you your food. Shall I give you some more? Some dal, Baba? Hey Dada, do you want more rice? Ma, what can I give you?'

'Did you cook for yourself?'

'You don't have to worry about me!' I would say, just the way Ma did on other days.

But what should I do right now? I observed Ma bringing down the areca bark one by one from the bamboo matting wall. What was she up to? 'The walls will become weak, Ma!'

'What can I do? Don't I have to light the stove?'

'Does that mean you'll remove the bark from the matting?'

'You're not well. Your Dada won't bring firewood. Baba's in his shop. So what am I supposed to do? Do you want me to use my limbs for fuel?'

I was silent. It's fine, let her do what she's doing. I would forage some bark later and put it up.

I was standing beside Ma. 'Aren't you going to school?' she asked.

'It's just reopened! Classes haven't started yet. Sir himself asks us to go home. He takes the attendance and then we're done. Besides, the booklist hasn't been given out yet. Once it's given, the books will have to be bought. Only after that will the school begin! Besides—'

'Besides what?' Ma looked at me and asked.

'The last time I got scabies, I attended school. Someone told Sir, and as soon as he entered the classroom, he sent me home. He said, "Come to school after your scabies has healed." What if he says that again?'

'Then come along to the hospital, it has to be treated, doesn't it? If it persists, you'll have to miss school. You'll fall behind.'

'Let's go then. You and I will go.'

I knew the scabies had to be treated. Apparently, it was communicable. Robi had complained. He would do that again now. Fine. Let it heal, I'll go to school after that, I thought. But could I afford to fall behind? Let the booklist come out, let me buy the books, and then I'll go on the first day of class.

Subol's house was near the marketplace. We were in the same class. I would take the booklist from him. I would copy it out. I would find out from him about those who had been promoted. It would be good if I could find someone nearby. But it didn't matter. I could even go to a house far away to get the old books at half-price. How far away could it be after all. I would go there and say, 'I've come to buy your old books!' He would bring them out. I would match them with the booklist and return home.

But what about the money? Wouldn't Baba provide that? He surely would. He got worried when something school-related had to be purchased, but he did buy it eventually. Baba hadn't been talking to me properly for a long time. As if I were to blame for all the problems at home. But I would still tell him. I had to. I thought, let a few days go by, let him become a bit cheerful, I'll tell him after that.

Suddenly one day, Baba took out something from his bag after he returned home at night. Something large. It was getting stuck at the mouth of the bag. A black-coloured bottle. I recognised it at once. It was a herbal medicine from Sadhana Aushadhalay, the shop in front of the courthouse. A tonic. Well done, Baba! I had been thinking of the same thing for the last few days, and then forgotten about it. Perhaps he read my thoughts and bought it. I had been thinking about taking Ma to the doctor and buying medicine for her. Baba had indeed done a great thing.

Ma wouldn't be unwell any more. She would feel cheerful. As soon as Baba freed the bottle from the opening of the bag and pulled it out, I took it from him and ran and placed it in Ma's lap. I said, 'Here! See what Baba has brought for you!'

But she didn't seem happy! Why was that? Why wasn't she saying anything? Didn't it make Ma happy? Was she cross with Baba? 'O Ma!'

'What?'

'Why aren't you saying anything?'

'What shall I say?'

'Baba bought you such good medicine!'

Ma said, 'Oh!'

I had not been to school for quite a few days. I was at home, and not going out anywhere either. I didn't like it. I observed everyone going to school, leaving the hamlet void. There was no one to play marbles with, no one from any house called out to Bhombol either. All I got to eat in the mornings was some chira or muri. Come lunchtime, I fetched a plate and sat down to eat all alone. Rice had been kept aside for me in a covered bowl. I sat all alone in the veranda of the kitchen and ate my lunch.

I wandered on the road. I plucked fragrant flowers. Like I wished to. What would they be used for? I didn't know that, yet I plucked them. The white flowers were so soothing to the eyes.

Baba returned the other day and suddenly pounced on me. He dragged me by my hair to the veranda. He said, 'Tell me why you aren't going to school!'

'O Baba, I'll go! O Baba … O Ma! Help me, Ma!'

'I'm going to kill you! From the shop I saw a crowd of students going to school, and you, my dear son, sit at home, playing make-believe games!' And at once he took the stick out from the roof truss and started hitting me on my back, arms and head.

'O Baba, I've cut my head, it's bleeding! O Baba! I'll go every day from now on!'

It seemed Baba wouldn't stop!

'Beat him! Feed poison to everyone and kill us all!' Ma sobbed out from inside.

Leave Right Now!

Other than what I was wearing, I only took the shirt and pants that I wore to school. I put those into the bundle in which I had packed an enamelled plate. If I ate at anyone's place, I would eat from that. There was a battered mug under the cot, should I take that? I wondered whether it would come in handy if I took it. I peeped into the room. The room was in darkness. I couldn't light a lamp either. Let it be. I wanted to take a gamchha, but there was only one at home. I pulled it down from the beam, but hung it back again.

Even the crows hadn't awoken. The vast field beside the Punti marsh shimmered when one looked at it on a blazing afternoon, but now before dawn it was completely still. The *kala-aam* mango tree behind the kitchen and the small mango plants were like shadowy clumps. I could only see the tint of the vitiligo-like marks on the trunks of the mango trees. Everything else was in darkness. Even this courtyard of alluvial clay seemed to be sleeping spreadeagled. A copper-coloured sky floated above.

What else? No, I wouldn't take my books. After all, I wasn't going to study any further. Chhor-da had studied till Class VI, and I till Class III. Ma had barely attended school, Baba hadn't either. Had Dadu, and the dadus before him, gone to school? There was no one in our community whom one could call educated. Let alone doing a job. I wanted to study a lot. But I had to suffer so much thrashing. Perhaps Baba wouldn't thrash me anymore if I worked and saved money and gave it to him.

Did Baba hit me of his own accord? Or did he do that only when he was unhappy on account of our poverty? I don't know. Why was I thinking so much when I was going to leave? I suddenly remembered that I had made vows at the tulsi pedestal and at the Kali temple. Although I had given up my studies, I would definitely make the offering to God that I had vowed to make. Wouldn't there be a tulsi pedestal or a temple where I was going?

I looked at Baba before leaving. A hazy figure lying on the floor of the veranda. Dada was beside him. Ma was lying on the side of the matting wall. Did anyone sense anything? It was cold. Everyone was asleep, wrapped up in their kanthas. I too had been under Ma's kantha. I got up quietly without anyone knowing. Us two brothers used the same kantha to keep ourselves warm. When he went somewhere, I gave it to him. When he was at home, it was folded and hung on the string. Let it be, I wouldn't take that either. If I took it, Dada wouldn't find it when he was going somewhere. He wouldn't be able to keep himself warm. What else could I take?

I exited the house and walked ahead too, but I suddenly felt an eerie sensation. I halted. Wasn't that a dead body from Bunopara being carried on a bamboo bier? *Bolo Hari!* I ran back home. Straight to the veranda. I was trembling. Should I go inside? No. What was there to be scared of in one's own house? Why had I spotted those people carrying the dead body? They were carrying it right in front of me. But I had never been struck like this by such a sight before, so why now?

I pushed open the shut door and peeped inside. No, I wouldn't look. I wouldn't feel like going if I did that. I wouldn't feel like leaving Ma behind. I had wanted to get admitted to the school near Ma's father's house. Ma had wanted to go too, but that didn't happen. So all of one's wishes don't come true! Would I get thrashed so much by Baba if they did? I put my hand on my left arm. Yes, the welts were still swollen. The flesh still felt hot and hard. And my head hurt if I touched my hair. Ma could have come and freed me. Why didn't she stop that? Did she too want Baba to beat me? I shut the door again quietly.

Was it dawn now? There was a pale light below the trees that had broken the darkness. Yes, it was dawn. I stepped down from the veranda again. I went outside. Ma woke up at dawn every day. She wouldn't let me go if she spotted me. Now that I was outside I no longer felt scared. Rather, I was keen to leave.

The road going past the banyan tree was visible now. My shirt and pants and the plate were packed in the bundle. And I was wearing a full-sleeved shirt and printed pants held up by a drawstring. The safety pin on the shirt was fastened. I had straightened my neck and fastened it intuitively when I stepped out into the cold. But it was not so cold now.

I knew where I was headed. I wouldn't tell anyone. Not many people knew the name of Bhabanhati, the place I was going to. One had to go southwards from our Magura. It was a nine-mile-long journey. If one went by bus, that was the one going to Aarpara. One had to get off at the iron bridge, and walk across a few fields to reach Bhabanhati. I knew the way by rote after having heard it from Chhor-da. Bhabanhati was where Baba went to get his scissors and razors sharpened. No one did that sharpening work here in our village. I didn't know anyone there. Dada had been there. 'What a great place, Bhai! With the Fotki river flowing alongside. Its waters are so crystal clear! Not at all like our river. The tiny waves seemed to be gleaming. The algae on its bank looked like a strip of ribbon. That swayed with the waves. How the dolphins somersaulted as one stood watching at the Kechodubi jetty!'

I had not seen dolphins. I had heard that they were there in our Madhumati river. That they could be spotted from time to time. But what Dada said was this: 'When the dolphins suddenly sprang out of the water and then plunged in again, it was as if a baby elephant had risen up in joy to see us.' It was the same Bhabanhati that I was going to. There was a big weekly market like ours in Aarpara. If I could stay in that village, it would be both far away from home as well as a fine place to live in. I knew I wouldn't get much money right away. I also knew that I would only get food at first. If I found work in a decent household, they might pay me a few taka too. I had no idea what the household would be like. I would tell them, 'Employ me, I'll do whatever you tell me. Household work, shop work, grazing cows and calves. I can do it all.'

I reached Bhaynar Mor. A motor bus was waiting there. Was it the bus going to Aarpara? A lot of people had boarded the bus and occupied the seats. A lot of people had also climbed atop the bus via the ladder at the rear. Sacks and bundles were also tied down on top. One man held a rooster in his hand. It could see everything below as it sat atop the bus. It kept darting its eyes this way and that. There was a boy who was slightly older than me. As soon as I approached him, he asked me, 'Are you going?'

I had my bundle in my hand. My feet were bare. I shook my head to say 'No'. I would walk. Was this Dada the helper? Must be. If he was the conductor, he would have had a leather bag on his shoulder. Did this Dada know Ashit? Should I ask him? Ashit is my friend. He works on a bus in Jessore. Do you know him?

I stood there observing the Dada. He was calling out to people. 'Get in, get in, the bus is leaving! Bhitesari, Jagla, Aarpara!' And as he said that, he banged the side of the bus. Seeing me looking at him, he took a few steps towards me. He asked, 'Where do you want to go? Where are you going with your bundle?'

'Bhabanhati.'

'Do you live there?'

'No.' And I walked ahead. I had a long way to go.

A few dogs were asleep with their snouts buried in their sides in the marketplace in Bhabanhati in the afternoon. Hearing me all of a sudden, they lifted up their heads to look. I tried to spot a shop selling food. I had only a few annas with me. I hadn't spent it on the way. I thought I would retain as much as possible. I would be full if I had a singhara and two jilipis. And two glasses of water. Wasn't even a single shop open? I came out of the tin-sheet marketplace. There was a river nearby! Was this the Fotki river? It was this river that Chhor-da had spoken of.

A shop was located in such a spot that it looked as if the kitchen waste and dirty water from it could simply be flung into the river. A man there was cleaning a rasogolla wok. Seeing me, he stopped and looked at me. After scrutinising me for a while, he returned to his cleaning. I figured out that what I wanted to eat wasn't available. A plate of danadar sweets was visible through the murky glass of the display case. *Kanchagola, paeda, sandesh*. I would feel nauseous if I ate sweetmeats on an empty stomach. And I didn't feel like having these things either. They must be expensive. If I spent all my money so soon …

'Can I get a glass of water please?'

Interrupting his wok cleaning, the man said, 'Look there, it's in the drum in front. Take it with the mug tied to a stick. There's a glass beside it.'

As I gulped down a few mouthfuls, I had a choking feeling. Was that because I drank water on an empty stomach? I returned to the tin-roofed marketplace. The dogs didn't lift their heads to look this time. I sat down, resting on a post. I had rested many times along the way. Yet my legs ached. Perhaps they wouldn't ache if I walked. My eyes were shutting. I was feeling sleepy. I dozed off.

I woke up to the prodding of a watchman's lathi. I shielded my eyes with my hand the moment he flashed his torch on my face. The man asked, 'Where are you from?'

His face was wrapped in a gamchha. I felt scared. My bundle was away from me, I pulled that to my side, and said, 'Dari Magura.'

'Dari Magura? Where's that?'

'Do you know Magura town? It's west of that. You know where the Haatkhola marketplace and the Kali temple are? It's past that. My house is near the banyan tree.'

'Why have you come here?'

'To work.'

'Work? You live near the town, there's lots of work there, and you've come to this remote village?'

Another watchman who stood beside him said, 'Check his pockets. Some big thief's sent him ... take him to the police station. Once the cane lands on him he'll blurt out everything.'

I fell at the other man's feet and began weeping.

'Tell the truth, what have you come here for?'

I told him everything. 'Baba beats me a lot. That's why I came away. I'll work and survive!'

Perhaps he believed me. 'Lie down. Didn't you bring a sheet?'

I was silent. The light from the torch was no longer on my eyes.

'Hey, you're wearing only a shirt in this cold weather?'

I continued to be silent.

'What does your father do?'

'He works as a barber.'

The man beside him said, 'I feel pity too, the boy is from a poor family. Sleep here, where can I take you at this time? We are the watchmen of this market. Have you eaten?'

Silence.

No, they didn't ask any more questions. There they were, walking away with their torches flashing.

I had never imagined that they would employ me at once. It was the second watchman who showed me a place to stay. There was a lot of vacant space next to the sacks of fodder beside the pile of straw in the cattle shed. He said, 'Spread out some straw there, it will feel like a mattress. I'll give you a kantha and a sheet. You can sleep comfortably.'

'Kaka, can you give me some water?'

'Yes … have you eaten?'

I lowered my head.

'Come, eat something first. You can start working after that.'

Did he mind my asking for food? What if he thought, how much he eats! Can I afford to feed him so much? I didn't ask again. But the man himself said, 'Wash your plate after eating, and keep it upside down there. Eat from that every day.'

I went to the cattle shed and kept the kantha and torn sheet that he gave me to spread out. I asked him, 'Do you want me to do anything?'

'Can you cut straw?'

'I can do it.'

'You don't have to do it now. You can go out for a walk if you feel like.'

Whatever Dada had said was all turning out to be true. There was a lot to see, especially the dolphins. It was really a spectacular sight! As I walked some more, I saw a ferry boat crossing the river with many people on it. 'Which village is it across the river, Chacha?'

'Bhatoyail. Taalkhori. Where do you want to go?'

'I'm not going anywhere. I've come to work in Bhabanhati village.'

My throat and chest were feeling parched with hunger. How blissful the prospect of food was! I felt like sleeping right away. On the grassy bank of the Futki river. But no, I didn't do that. It was a new place. I thought, I would roam around some more once I became familiar with the place. I would come by to watch the dolphins.

The man had given a kantha and a sheet. I took out the plate from my bundle. I would eat from that. I would wash it after that, and keep it upside down here. The man came and smoked the cattle shed with resin. Were there a lot of mosquitoes? I hadn't noticed last night. I was so sleepy! It was pitch dark in the straw store. A few fireflies were flying around in a wave pattern, as if they were stitching something. I gazed at their glowing light.

When the man brought me my food, he said, 'You must wake up early in the morning. Bring the cows out as soon as you wake up. I'll come and show you. Eat up, and go to sleep quickly. Hey, I don't even know what your name is!'

I told him. And then I began eating. He served some more rice and vegetable curry in the middle of the plate. I continued eating. 'Could I get some salt please?'

'You have so much salt!'

What was Ma doing? Was she crying? Did Baba say anything to Ma about me when he returned home yesterday? What could he have said? Or had Ma become even more unwell because I had left? I didn't feel sleepy after I finished my meal. I kept thinking about home, about Baba's shop and about going from house to house looking for books to buy at half-price. 'You shouldn't have come so late! I've already sold the books!'

After that, I imagined I had gone and stood beside Robi's pit. There were large leaves of taro around the pit. I went closer and sprayed my urine on the leaves.

The man called out to me in the morning. 'Hey Ratan, wake up!'

I didn't wake up right away. I stretched lazily and turned to the other side. He called out again, this time accompanied by a shake. 'Hey, wake up!'

He didn't say anything, but he sniffed. He came closer. He sniffed again, and said, 'Did you piss in bed?'

I realised that my pants and the kantha were all wet. I sat up in silence and shame.

'Hey, go back home! Leave just now, you wretched fellow! You don't have to work here!'

It was just as well. How I had missed Ma all night.

Once the man left, I packed the shirt and pants that I wore to school and the plate inside the cloth bundle. Once I packed that, I left wearing the same pair of wet pants.

The dawn was exactly as it had been the day before yesterday. Crows were calling from the roof. Fortunately I hadn't spent the four annas I had taken with me. I would take the motor bus to Magura. Wouldn't four annas be enough? Let me get in first. If the conductor asked for more, I'd say, 'But it's half-price for students.'

We had left Bhabanhati and arrived close to the iron bridge. It would probably be afternoon by the time I reached home. Afternoon was the time that Ma and I spent together at home.

OUR VILLAGE, OUR HOUSE

Jhulir Bagan

The place called Jhulir Bagan, or Jhuli's Garden, was a frightening one. One shivered in fear even in the daytime, there was no saying what it would be like at night. But there was only a single route to the fields for foraging! Yes, one could take an alternative route, but it was a very circuitous one. No one went by Jhulir Bagan all alone during the day. They were always in pairs, or in a group. As one approached the place, one's whole body seemed to turn leaden. There might be titters of laughter at any moment. *Hee hee!* Your name might be called out too! 'Hey Kishto, come here!'

Kishto, a pet name. That's how everyone in the village pronounced the name. A simple, colloquial name. You turned around and looked, but there would be no one. Who was it that walked around in the garden? The sound of leaves rustling was heard in the silent afternoon. A few days back, on the topmost branch, there was someone in a red-bordered sari. I heard about all that in the gathering under the banyan tree. All kinds of tales. Ghost stories. Tales of thieves. Someone had got the smell of cooking too from the dense jungle. Apparently, it was like the smell of rotten fish. So that was Jhulir Bagan. There were so many mangoes, the colour of sindoor, hanging there, beyond the reach of stones. Mango-pluckers too didn't want to go there. What if someone crept up from behind!

Who crept up from behind?

Who else? The ghost!

A female ghoul?

She'll be there too! Ghosts and ghouls, and their children. They pluck grapefruits and play football with them. There's also a school for the little ghosts. Apparently if one listens carefully, you can hear their voices. 'A for apple!'

Jhulir Bagan was a hamlet of ghosts near our village. People said that they could not be spotted during the day, but there was no guarantee that you wouldn't encounter them either. Apparently, they were dazzled when sunlight fell on the pupils of their sunken eyes. It was on cloudy days, when the sun was not visible, that they moved about. The rustle of leaves. Apparently, they're terribly scared of fire. People say they're scared of iron too. I couldn't figure out why they were scared of iron. But yes, one could brandish a chopper made of that, they ought to be scared on seeing that. They ought to be scared if one advanced with a spear at the ready. They might get scared if one threatened them with a *bonti* knife. Why on earth did ghosts get scared? Anyway, there's no need to talk about all that. What's the point in dwelling upon the errors of stupid ghosts? One had to go along that path, and so one needed to travel safely. If one carried iron, no ghost would come near, and so one ought to do that.

The hamlet of ghosts was right across the canal, after Bunopara, the hamlet of the pig-herding folk. How could it be that you went along that way and didn't get scared? If one didn't get scared, the very term 'ghostly' would become a lie. There were so many people here long ago, there were houses, but if one said that now it would seem like a fairytale. 'There was a story, it had three heads/It put its head in the garden of cane/That's the end of my fairy tale.' These were the kinds of ditties regarding fairytales that had spread in the village. That's where we belonged. I spent my childhood in that village in East Bengal. I never knew of any fairytales. It was only after I arrived in Calcutta that I learnt about them. Fairytales. Demons and monsters. The tale of the marriage of a fairy prince and a fairy princess. Crossing the seven seas astride a winged horse. Travelling endlessly. Stories like that. But in our village, we had Jhulir Bagan, and the field beside the marsh known as Punti. There was the lakeside. And horse-drawn carriages.

It wasn't too far away from our house. It took about thirty minutes if one walked. Jhulir Bagan lay in the direction one faced while standing at the lakeside with your back to Pireni Ma's house. The place was wrapped in mist. If one advanced slowly, the mist parted and there were shrubs and bushes and tall trees. As soon as one spotted creepers with hanging vines, one had to be on the alert as it was the edge of Jhulir Bagan.

We friends huddled together as we walked, with the metal ballast for the fishing net, which was supposed to protect one from ghosts and ghouls, tucked into our waist strings. And an amulet from Kala Sadhu on one's forearm, perils begone! But despite all that, one was still sacred. No one spoke. We tread carefully.

Our old house was just opposite this edge of Jhulir Bagan. That was before Mej-da was born. Baba had subsequently removed the bamboo posts and made our present house beside the banyan tree near the riverbank. I've heard that all the people in that village inside the dense forest left one by one, and began building houses near the marketplace in Magura. Bor-da was a little boy then. Ma was scared. She told Baba about it too. But Baba paid no heed. Meaning, on account of money. Baba used to go out for work to marketplaces and towns four or five miles away. In towns, he would go from house to house seeking custom.

People used to come from far-flung places to hang themselves in Jhulir Bagan. Things like that happened in the village. A bit of scolding or a trivial altercation with folks at home was enough to make someone set out with a length of rope, because of their wounded pride. They chose a faraway place to avoid the risk of anyone sensing something if they went nearby. A secluded garden with no people nearby. Only trees! Debtaru trees and clumps of bamboo next to one another had made the garden densely wooded. There was a rattan grove too within that. And mango, jamun and persimmon trees as well. But I never ventured there. After all, I was born in the new house. I learnt about the fear when I was older, when I joined school. Some people said that the garden belonged to weavers. Others said there was a young woman named Jhuli, and that it was her garden. That it was named after her. Had Jhuli hung herself there?

Poor folk were less afraid; only they went there to cut bamboo poles. They used them for making posts and matting. It was the year 1964. The price of a bamboo pole was one-and-a-half taka. Where on earth would they get so much money. It was so difficult for them to even buy rice at six annas a seer. Their daily wages were three taka or less. People lived in the forest notwithstanding their fear. People live in such places even now. They could not imagine having a shelter near a marketplace or town. And so they built tiny huts with grass thatch in fields and forests. We too had such a house. The saplings planted in that abandoned site had grown into giant trees that were turning old now. The place was a jungle.

The closest hamlet to that was Bunopara. The people there grazed pigs and goats. *Hei ho!* They raised chickens that kept busy foraging and crowing. *Kukurukoo!* Tiny huts behind lath fences. Womenfolk going with clay pitchers, with a ghomta over their heads and faces. When they returned with water, they slanted to one side, with the other arm swinging up and down. The tubewell was a mile-and-a-half away. Jhulir Bagan was a short distance away from this hamlet. After we left the place, vines and creepers grew on the path and concealed it altogether. But the path was still visible because of the bullock carts. The heavy wheels of the cart did not allow grass or undergrowth to remain. The winding line of the path encircled by the jungle seemed to spin a web of mystery. All other gardens belonged to people, but this was entirely for the ghosts. It belonged to Jhuli. I had never seen such a desolate place close to any village nearby. In the midst of all that, news would suddenly spread, or someone would spot a person or a young woman hanging from a branch of a mango tree. On the morning of one such day, Baba had set out from home and returned. He said to Ma, 'I feel bad. Bishe's boy hung himself.'

People had been living in fear for long. Ma said, 'Everyone has left. Look for a plot of land. I feel very scared here. I'm alone here with the little boy, all day. What if something happens?'

Baba heard her. But he didn't say anything. A few days later, he sold off the land with the paan-yard, and bought our present plot. On which the house I was born in was built. Though we made a new house, our old homestead remained. We called it our ‘garden’ now. Whenever I went past it, I wondered, was there a house in this garden?

There was no fence. It just lay there. Ma left us some days back. Baba had sold off this garden because Ma had asked him to. Not because Ma was ill, but in order to build a shop for my Bor-da and Mej-da. Baba had taken me there after he sold it. He had planted a few mango saplings there. Those had grown into big trees. They would probably bear fruit the next year. I placed my hand on the dark mango leaves. Tiny insects made a buzzing sound and flew off the leaf. There were lots of arum plants below the tree. I asked Baba, ‘Ma loved this, isn’t it Baba?’

Baba looked at me. But he didn’t say anything. I busied myself plucking the leaves and stems. Within a short time, I had gathered quite a few bundles. I continued plucking. Baba asked, ‘What will you do with so many?’

I stopped.

Baba walked ahead. There was an elevated spot. He went atop that. He looked much taller than me now. I observed that as I plucked the arum. He was going around the spot like I would. He then got down. He placed his hand on a big mango tree. He stroked the trunk a few times with his fingers. He had become strangely silent. Why did he stroke the tree?

I stopped plucking the arum and went to Baba. I didn’t have to say anything. Baba said, ‘Come, let’s go back now.’

The bundles of arum were tied with vines. We walked side by side. Baba did not say a single word. I wanted to look at his face. Sensing that, I don’t know why he kept turning his face away. Was he crying?

Baba had sold the garden to Maulana Mati. He was a clerk in the court. Maulana saheb’s house was near that of Nilu the washerman. In Jolapara, the weavers' hamlet. The azaan sounded there. *Allahu Akbar!* Just before dusk, the sound from the loudspeaker fixed atop a bamboo pole spread far and wide. I had seen Maulana Mati walking along the lake. Our garden belonged to him now.

Was that why Baba kept looking back? To see where the bedroom was. And the kitchen. Was that why he paused from time to time as he walked? He said, 'Ratan, that paan-yard used to belong to us.'

I looked, holding the pile of arum in my hands. 'Does that too belong to Maulana Mati now?'

'No, it's a person from Batkedanga, you don't know him.'

'Let's go home. I'm not coming here again now that I've seen it once.'

I had not gone foraging in the fields for a long time. My friends called out to me. But I shook my head. 'I'm not going, you people go.'

I wandered around all by myself. I sat in the thicket of reeds at the riverbank and watched the water hyacinths float along the river. A kingfisher hung suspended in the air. Its wings fluttered as it gazed into the water. And then a splash. It dove into the water and rose up again, yes, it had a fish in its beak, and it flew away with a chirp. Did it have chicks? Was it going to feed them? Would they open their tiny beaks? As I observed all that quietly, I remembered Ma. I thought she would arrive now and call me, 'Ratan, come to eat!'

I began going to the fields again. I went every alternate day. There were three or four houses in our hamlet. Besides our house, there were Ashit, Shyama and Putu's houses. Putu's father, Sudarshan Kaka, weighed paddy at the weekly market. 'It's one basket, it's two baskets ...' he counted aloud as he weighed. The basket was a large one, made of rattan. Paddy was measured by the basket. Sudarshan Kaka was paid when the market closed. Ashit's father took rice from the *mahajan* and set up shop. He got money if he managed to sell it.

Shyama's father and my Baba went from house to house for work. They didn't have any cultivable land. That's why we kids foraged the fields. For dry twigs and cow dung. I set out with a sack and an axe. I went very far as I foraged. All the way to the weekly market known as Hauder Haat. There was a wooden bridge next to that. And past the bridge was the Raotara School. On some days the school would be humming. 'Look, there's a motor bus!' I gazed at it, with the sack slung over my shoulder. The motor bus came steadily along from far away, astonishing us. Every now and then it was concealed by trees. And then it emerged in the sunlight again. It moved slowly. It went to Jhineda and Jessore. To Jessore town. 'Slowly, there are children!' the conductor would call out.

I didn't merely forage for cow dung—I observed all this too. When I climbed up from the field onto the metalled road and put my hand on the telephone post, how cool it was! It was like the cool paving in the government hospital. What were the sounds? I put my ear to the post and listened. Was it the sound of words? One couldn't make out. Did the words that travelled make such a sound as they went from pole to pole? It seemed like they were running. What were the words? 'Hello! Are you well?' 'Look after Ma!' 'Is that the SDO's office?'

The cable was overhead. It rested on a white stone shaped like a glass. Where did the sound come from? Was it from Jessore? Or Khulna? Or Dhaka? Didn't it come from India? Was it India, or Calcutta? It was all the same. It was thanks to the cable that the telephone in the post office rang. Could I speak on that? Ashit and company were sitting in the shade of the babla tree. I wrapped my arms around the pole. I placed my ear on it, then looked this way and that. No, there was no one. That's when I hugged the pole. 'Ma, this is Ratan! Can you hear me?'

I was silent. What was Ma doing now? Khurima had said, 'Don't be naughty, or else your Ma will feel sad. Remember, your Ma can see everything.' But where would she see me from? Khurima didn't tell me that. I called out again, 'Ma, o Ma!'

Why were my eyes turning moist?

No, they weren't my words, they belonged to other people. Perhaps it was their words that were travelling. I couldn't hear Ma's voice. My tears were on the post, I wiped them. And my eyes too. And as I wiped my tears, I descended once again to the boundary ridge on the field below. They probably hadn't seen my crying from so far away. I descended slowly, holding the dung sack in my hand.

What came over me at times? I thought of Ma when saying something or the other, no matter where I might be. It happened whenever I was alone. I felt like talking to Ma.

I had once brought a puppy from Ashit's house. There were many of them in the haystack. As soon as I had asked Ashit, he said, 'Take one along.'

The puppies wriggled to their mother's breast. They were white and cream-coloured. I liked the one with a reddish streak on its brow. I pointed to it. Is that why its mother looked directly at me? Did she understand what we said? I looked at her, she didn't take her eyes off me. Budho signalled to me with his eyes: A little later. She'll go out just now, just let someone call out, 'Come!' She'll run out at once. Just wait a bit.

That puppy grew up. I named him Bhombol. It accompanied me wherever I went. One day I asked him, 'Shall we go to one place?'

It tried to understand me, wagging its tail eagerly.

'Come. You're not afraid, are you?'

It's tail seemed to turn quiet.

'Hey, aren't I there!'

I ran from the paddy-threshing room to the road. I had an axe. As I reached the road, I thumped his back. 'Come!'

I was going to the fields for foraging after a long time. Before I left the house, I latched the room quietly. There wasn't anything to steal, but still. It had become a habit before leaving the house.

Bhombol and me. We walked a bit. After a while, I said, 'Run now.' And it was the two of us then. Just as we were going down to the canal bank, Pireni Ma called out, 'Hey Ratan, where are you going?'

She was very close to Ma. The two of them chatted quite often. She stopped me. 'Where are you going, boy?'

'I'm going to forage in the fields, Khurima!'

'Didn't I tell you not to go out by yourself for a month?'

Pireni Ma hadn't told me what would happen if I went out. She had said it in the same way that everyone in the hamlet had said things. Could one remember everything? And how much of that could one heed? Everyone was giving me a lot of love on account of Ma's departure. I stood there with my rolled-up sack, looking at Pireni Ma. She said, 'Stay at home for a month. Let the month be over, after that—'

'Can I go today? I came out with a lot of hope.'

Pireni Ma walked towards me. Her sari was dirty. Grimy and stained, just like Ma's. Her hair was dishevelled. It seemed like she was going to tell me something.

Bhombol was standing on the slope of the embankment. He observed Pireni Ma advancing with his tongue hanging out. From quite afar, she said, 'Come here!'

When I neared her, she stroked my head. After my head had been shaved, a crop of hair was growing on my scalp like tiny seedlings sprouting from paddy seeds. Pireni Ma asked, 'Why are you wandering about here and there?'

'There's no cow dung at home. Or fuelwood.'

'No my dear, don't go.' She held my hand and took me towards her house. 'I have a bundle of branches, take some. Don't go, my dear! It's not safe in those parts.'

I looked at Bhombol. He wagged his tail.

'Alright. Since you're saying ...' As I made to leave, Pireni Ma held my arm again. 'Do you want to eat something?'

Bhombol didn't dare to get excited. There was a small clump of bamboo beside the road. Pireni Ma's hut slanted down next to that. She lived all alone. She worked in a few households. She had her meals there. She only cooked at night. The hut had matted bamboo lath walls, a grass-thatch awning, and a veranda on a plinth which was about a foot high from the ground. Bhombol whimpered. I said to him, 'Wait.'

‘Does he eat muri?’

‘No. The devil doesn’t want to eat, he wants me to come along, that’s why he’s calling me.’

‘Alright, go then. Collect dry leaves from inside your hamlet itself. There’s no more fear of ghosts after some days.’

We left the place. Homewards again. I thumped Bhombol on his back, and said, ‘Come!’

Bhombol raced ahead in competition with me.

Wouldn’t We Have a House Anymore?

I woke up all of a sudden. Wasn’t that the sound of a snake catching a frog? Yes, that’s what it was like. It must be somewhere nearby. The frog was crying out repeatedly, and so my sleep was—there it is again! A muted scream. *Chyaan* … semi-daylight, semi-darkness. The light-and-darkness wafted in through the gaps and holes in the bamboo-matting wall. The frog continued to shriek. As if to say, is anyone there? *Chyaan!*

After all, the snake was swallowing it bit by bit. The frog was dying to leap out. But how could it do that? Wasn’t it caught in the maw! Perhaps it would enter the stomach in a little while. Was it a rat snake? Or a cobra? I had never heard a snake’s cry before. Snakes went around looking for frogs and mice in gardens and courtyards. There was only the sound of it slithering. The rustle of dry leaves.

Where was it? Beneath the lemon tree? At the base of the mango tree? Or had it come upon the frog right at the entrance and caught it? I was drowsy. I would get up once it had finished swallowing the frog. What if it spotted me and thought I had come to snatch its food, and then got angry, dropped the frog and struck me instead. I thought about all that too. One didn't hear the sound of a snake catching a frog very much in the month of Magh. But it had found one today. The frog must have been hopping along in front of it, and the snake did not tarry. The frog's crying was a lot less now. *Cheen*. Perhaps the snake too was hurrying. It knew that there was a bamboo grove right across. With mongoose burrows in the soil. If the snake sensed any kind of danger, it would probably let go of the frog. Was the frog calling the mongooses with its cry?

Ashit and I had once entered the mango orchard of the Dutta household to fetch dry branches. We were searching for dry twigs in the undergrowth there. Suddenly, Ashit screamed out, 'Hey Ratan, look, there's a snake!' I ran towards him, as if to grab it. But I stumbled on my sack and fell. Ashit helped me up, and said, 'There's nothing to be afraid of, look there, it's fighting with a mongoose.'

I looked. The snake was brownish in colour. Its hood was raised knee-high and swaying. And in front of it was the mongoose, observing it closely with its red-brown eyes, to see how it could grab its head. The mongoose leapt. The snake hissed and struck. The mongoose leapt again. Ashit pulled me by my arm, and said, 'Let's go, it's not safe to be here.'

The snake and the mongoose were face to face in the shadows. It was the first time I had seen such a confrontation. I had heard that if a mongoose spotted a snake it ran into the forest. It took the root of a particular tree in its mouth and then jumped upon the snake. The snake was cut to bits by that. But I hadn't seen this for myself. I had only heard about it. But there seemed to be an eternal enmity between the snake and the mongoose. Is that why the term 'snake-mongoose relationship' was in currency?

If I woke up before dawn and went out, I saw lots of snakes. I remembered Ma. If she had been around, she would have warned me for sure. She would have said, 'Don't step out at all, my dear.' That's why I continued to lie in bed. All by myself. I didn't feel like coming out from under my kantha. And with what was happening outside, there was no question of it.

In winter, the warmth of the kantha brought comfort to the grass-thatched room every night. How cold I would be before getting into bed. I wrapped myself in the kantha like a bundle. The cold seemed to disappear after that. But it hovered around. It only left once I had fallen asleep. I don't know whether it swore at me before it left.

The frog's *chyaan* seemed to have lessened. I would get up once it stopped altogether. I feared that it might be a poisonous snake. Anyway, it would go away in a little while through the ditch at the rear. But what if it entered the house instead? I kept my eyes peeled. What if it entered the house through some opening, and slithered over some utensil which then fell with a crash? I didn't blink. There was complete silence inside the house at daybreak. Not a single sound other than my own.

The earth under the rear door had receded bit by bit, leaving a gaping hole. It looked like an opening. What if the snake entered through that? I heard the sound of a snake catching a frog at least a couple of times a day in the rainy season. Frogs croaked to their hearts' content. Rain poured, flooding the earth. It seemed that all the frogs of the village had come to our hamlet to croak. *Gyan-goan ... kiri kiri.*

It was through the opening under my door that one day a jackal, with a couple of its cubs in tow, had peeped in. Ma noticed everything. She had screamed out that night despite her gasping lungs, 'Hey Ratan! Wake up! Look, something peeped in from the hole!'

Baba got up noisily. He lit the lamp. I saw a jackal with a couple of cubs standing on the path beside the bamboo thicket. We started shouting. Looked for a stone and flung it. The stone probably didn't hit the jackal, but it ran into the bamboo grove. Baba returned to the house, and said, 'I get it. They came because there was a ripe jackfruit at home that had been cut open.'

Stuffing a sack into the hole under the door, Baba said, 'I need to fill it up with earth quickly.'

Baba hadn't closed the hole as yet. None of us had sensed that Ma would go so soon. Ever since then, our house bore a kind of vagabond look. The hole under the door was gaping like before. It had been so many days since the courtyard had been swept with a broom. I didn't feel like using the broom either. There was a heap of leaves from the guava tree that had fallen in one corner of the courtyard. The leaves on the clay courtyard had got wet in the dew and begun to rot. But there was no odour. A brown bird turned over the leaves and pulled out tiny earthworms every morning.

Baba had been cooking for many days. If you could call it cooking! On most days it was rice gruel with mashed jackfruit seeds, a chilli, a few drops of mustard oil, and salt. The rice tasted sweet when eaten with the jackfruit seeds. The final dregs of starch remained in the clay rice pot. I scraped it off with my hand. My nails scraped against the pot, making a noise. Sticky rice starch. If I got rice, I didn't need anything else. After helping himself, Baba would push the pot towards me. He knew I liked the starch. If Ma had been around, she would have said, 'You shouldn't scrape off rice and eat it.' She used to do it herself and give it to me. But since Ma wasn't there, Baba did not chide me. He pushed the pot towards me. I scraped off the starch and ate it to my heart's content.

The number of Baba's customers had dwindled. He used to return home to feed Ma from an enamelled plate. He sat beside Ma, who lay near the door. 'Like to eat a bit of rice?'

Ma would shake her head. 'No, I can't eat that.'

Yet he held the plate in front of her, just in case she felt like eating.

Feeding her rice, giving her the tonic from Kundeshwari Pharmacy, there was none of that any more. So Baba did some cooking, using this and that. He left for work after feeding us. He never said a word while eating. He no longer told me to study either. He did so many chores at home when Ma was around. Right at dawn came the swishing sound of the courtyard being swept, to the accompaniment of the chanting of the Lord's name in melody. Baba would wake up the whole household with his song. But he didn't do all that either now. He had suddenly become like an old man. What had happened to Baba?

Bhombol observed the chores in the morning from the courtyard of the house. It watched a bird sit. Fly away. If the crows cawed too loudly, he barked, *gheu gheu*, and made to leap from under the awning, frightening and forcing them to fly away. As if the responsibility for looking after the house rested upon him.

He lay curled up beside the steps with his face snuggled against his belly. Every now and then he chased fleas, snapping his jaws at them. He got annoyed and pounced on them. But he couldn't catch them; if he could, he would have chewed them to bits. It was because he couldn't that he made the sound of teeth gnashing. His failure probably upset him. He looked this way and that once again. He observed where they perched, on his tail and shoulder. He spent his time in this manner. He didn't do anything else besides that. He too seemed to have turned silent like Baba. He knew that I would appear with a lump of rice at the right time. Did Bhombol realise that we were not like we were before? How different we had become from how we had once been.

Baba gave him rice but only rarely. It was only I who fed him. In fact I gave him a little extra. It was fine if I ate a bit less, I was happy as long as Bhombol ate enough. Besides, from the time he had been a pup he almost never went to any other house. That's why when he went out on the road, the dogs in the neighbourhood didn't accept him very well. Was that because he received affection from the neighbours as he accompanied me? Or was it because I didn't allow him to be with them?

I couldn't go very far when he accompanied me. It was risky to go past other hamlets. The dogs there kept growling. One had to carry a big stick. The stick came in handy the moment the dogs spotted Bhombol and advanced to bite him. Once they got a tight thwack, they whimpered, *kyaon kyaon*, and fled. They went afar and began barking again. They observed the stick swinging in my hand. They didn't move—only the sound of barking would be heard. I protected Bhombol like that as we made our way. The other day I was taking him along the path leading to Jhulir Bagan. There was no habitation on the way other than in Bunopara. Pireni Ma lived in such a wooded location that dogs never ventured there. And why would they when there wasn't the slightest smell of any cooking wafting out of her house? She wouldn't let me go even as I set off. She was very close to Ma. I didn't disregard her. Doing that would mean hurting someone close to Ma.

After we had eaten at night, I spread a torn sack in a corner by the steps, and Bhombol lay down on it. Perhaps, it had woken up by now. No, there was no more sound coming from the frog. Where had the snake gone? Anyway, let it go wherever it wished to.

After all, we lived with them. This village, this hamlet. That's why I wasn't really scared. Foxes, jackals, hornets, bees, scorpions, caterpillars—and so much more. Could one imagine the village without them? To each his own. Such was our village, our house.

I was lying in bed lazily. I had woken up to the sound of the snake catching a frog. And then I thought about various things. And I had dozed off in the process. Fine strands of sunlight were coming in through the gaps in the bamboo-matting. Baba and Chhor-da had left without me. Chhor-da now went to work with Baba. He was learning the trade. Cutting hair and shaving beards. He didn't want to go, but Baba forced him to do so. So he left with Baba at dawn despite his unwillingness. I knew there was rice in the pot. It could be left out in the winter. Once I was a little older I would be able to cook rice myself. I would cook something after waking up at dawn. If I did that, Baba and Dada wouldn't have to leave for work on an empty stomach, or after having eaten only fermented rice.

I had observed Ma cooking so many times. To cook rice, one had to pour water into the pot up till a hand's width above the level of the rice grains. The rice would cook very nicely then. After dancing around in joy and playing for quite a while, when the rice finally began boiling, and the lid on the pot began to tremble, that was it. Ma used to remove the lid and then blow on her scorched fingers. She could use her anchal to lift it, but she thought that would be polluting, and so she used her hands. It wasn't about rice grains but cooked rice that the notion of pollution existed in our village. Wherever there was the soiling touch of consumed food, it had to be washed clean. If one touched food with one's sari, one had to change the sari. Ma didn't have so many saris, did she? But I wouldn't be able to lift the lid off the pot like Ma did. I know Ma did not like greasy rags, but since she wasn't around, I would take the pot off the stove using rags. Wouldn't I be able to do that?

So many thoughts crossed my mind. Ma had made me into a big boy before going. I used to go to the riverbank all by myself and wash the utensils. We didn't have any bowls. Ma used to serve all the items on the plate itself. Baba too did the same. We owned only a few enamelled plates. So there weren't too many utensils to wash.

My pair of black shorts, held to my waist with a string, swayed this way and that as I walked towards the riverbank. Bhombol would amble alongside me. The devil accompanied me everywhere. But I couldn't do my work as soon as I reached there. There would be lots of people there. I had to stand and await my turn. The others there did not let me sit there lest

I splashed water on them. We belonged to a low caste. The womenfolk would have to bathe afresh if water from my hands touched them. I stood waiting because I knew that. I moved away from the jetty. I sat down to wash the utensils only after the others had finished washing theirs.

It was just as well. Once the crowd left, the murky water became clear. The sandy bank sparkled again. One could see strings of algae swaying in the depths. Chyalo fish peeped from behind the algae. When the sorputi fish swirled their bodies, I felt like touching their silver bellies. They glistened even more in the sunlight when the riverbank was desolate. So many fish came to eat the leftover rice washed off the plates because I was alone. When the bele fish arrived, they puffed themselves up and looked me in the eye. It was great fun. I observed their antics silently. There would be very little leftover rice on my plate, yet they darted forward. Their arrival meant 'Give us something, Ratan Dada!'

After dipping the plates in the water, I kept gazing at them. I whiled away my time doing that. But there wasn't any more rice. They gobbled up whatever little there was. They wanted more. They nibbled at my fingers in the water, as if asking, where's the rice? That felt ticklish. There wasn't any, but they didn't want to leave. I simply observed them. Being considered repugnant had its advantages. One could be all alone. And when one was alone these were the creatures that became one's friends. The fish in the river, the crows on the trees. I enjoyed imitating the crows. I felt like I was talking to them. They cawed again, *Cr-a-a!*

I splashed the water as I washed the utensils. The crows hopped away, then returned again. They understood that I was playing with them. If I sat there for too long, it was Bhombol who called out, '*Aaown!* What's up, Dada, aren't you going to school?'

That's right.

The two of us returned home. I didn't feel like going to school these days. Perhaps I too would leave school like Chhor-da. I felt unhappy all the time after Ma's death. I felt unsettled. Ma seemed to be peeping out from behind the lines of the books, whether it was day or night. She still seemed to be saying, 'Listen to your Baba. Listen to your Dadas, my dear!' That's why I felt unsettled when I was all alone at home. I stepped out. Bhombol would be asleep with his face snuggled in his belly. I felt restless. I called out loudly to my friends to come to play. 'Hey Haran! Like to play motor bus? There's a pile of wood under Dipu's jackfruit tree, come let's go and play motor bus. Climb up to a log, hold a branch, and then—zoom! To Jhineda, Jessore and Dhaka. "Who wants to go? Get in, get in!" That game.' And sometimes it was playing with hanging ropes. As if everyone in the hamlet had been called and teams had been formed. But no one called me. They had been asked not to by their folks, and so they didn't hang around with me. They didn't include me in their games. Thank God for Bhombol. It was he who was my playmate now. He meant everything to me. On the days I went to school, I patted him on his head before I left. That made him terribly happy. Perhaps he inwardly said, 'Go Dada, don't worry, I'm here!' And when I returned home again, I found Bhombol still lying there. How much work did Baba and Dada do in comparison?

Baba said that our house was on an eighteen-*kattha* plot. There were only two rooms. One was roofed with grass-thatch, the other had a tin-sheet roof. There was a paddy-threshing shed too. That's where I laid the dry leaves, twigs and cow dung. I wasn't allowed there now because snakes nested there. It was full of cobwebs. With colourful spiders. They had huge legs. Their legs were very poisonous. If they scratched you somewhere, the spot became sore. The thresher lay lengthwise in the shed. Mustard used to be ground here earlier. And turmeric. Rice was flattened here as well. All this had not happened for so long. After Ma fell ill, the threshing shed fell into disuse. The bamboo posts of this shed had been damaged by termites and had become wobbly and slanted. The space around the shed was full of mango, jamun and guava trees and taro plants. I remember the house had been surrounded by a lath fence. That wasn't there anymore either. Termites had attacked the laths, and they had given way and fallen to the ground. Cows and goats entered the compound at ease. They entered without a care and left after grazing.

Branches grew from trees, and vines and creepers grew and spread from one branch to another. Perhaps after some time our house would not be recognisable any more. There would be so much of jungle all around that we too would feel scared to enter. The morning glory and toothbrush plants had joined their vines and branches and virtually surrounded us. One day I heard that Baba was going to sell off this house too. He was saying something to Chhor-da, and when he spotted me he fell silent. I thought I heard him say that he would sell the house. Wouldn't we have a house anymore? Where would we go then?

The Market Contractor's Rent

There wasn't a single vacant plot in the fields. The tender stalks were ready for harvesting. They were mostly mustard flowers. There was a bit of chickpea and lentil. Some shon-grass that was used for thatch. But it was mostly mustard. The plots measured two or three katthas. Some people had a bit more. The flowers appeared at first, and then the fruits. Fruit meaning chickpea, lentil, and mustard. Sparkling yellow flowers, which concealed the other crops. It looked as if a sandy bank of yellow had emerged in the middle of the Syaosganti lake. How had such a change taken place in the few days that I had not gone to the fields to forage for cow dung?

The tender stalks were shining in the sunlight. A bird flew by. It seemed to be flying over a sea of yellow. Walking through the field now meant walking on the boundary ridge. Tiny snail shells on the path. Burrows of mice. Fish eggs retrieved by mice lay on the earth in places. As I stood on the path carpeted with grass, I couldn't see any cows or goats sent to graze. There was still the glitter of dew on the yellow flowers though it was late morning. No, I wouldn't find any dry cow dung here, yet I walked on. I felt like walking. I moved ahead cautiously. If I was unmindful, I would fall from the ridge onto the field. My knotted sack was under my arm.

I had never come here by myself. Ashit was usually with me. And Shyama. They had called me earlier. I hadn't gone. I had been forbidden to leave the house for a month after the ritual impurity cast by Ma's death. Pireni Ma had said, 'You mustn't step out at all after dusk.' Baba had not really said anything. Since Ma was not there, I did not leave the house. I couldn't help thinking that Ma was present in every part of the house. Leaving the house meant leaving Ma's things unattended. So I wandered around within the house itself. I sat beside the stove in the kitchen. On the wooden floor-seat on which Ma sat while cooking. I picked up the lamp covered in grease and dust and gazed at it. And then I got up. The sweater from Bhutan that Baba used to wrap around Ma everyday had not been put away and still lay in the main room. One day he said, 'She wore this in her final days, isn't it, you should keep it.' I immediately wore the sweater. I sniffed it. And then I put it away.

I seemed to have forgotten about school altogether. I gazed at the narrow bamboo bridge at school time. Beneath that was the Nabaganga. Rows of boats were anchored there on the market days. The image of the Class III Sir walking along ... Everything floated before my eyes. But it was only the last bench for me. However early I arrived at school, the front bench was not for me even if it was empty. That had been continuing from the time I was in Class I. We had to sit on the floor in Class I. There were benches from Class II onwards. Class I meant the rectangular room at the riverbank, which had no walls and only a tin-sheet roof over bamboo posts. That was Class I. I had pus in my ears then. I used to get that in winter time. I used to get scabies too. I wore underpants with a drawstring. And a shirt purchased at the weekly market. The boys didn't let me sit with them because Baba did dirty work. But that didn't matter. Eventually they asked me to sit further away. I did that. That had its advantages. Sir did not ask me anything. So I didn't get a thrashing on that account. He only thrashed me when the others made false complaints against me. I never screamed. Didn't quarrel either.

But I had still got admitted to school, hadn't I? I was in Class II now. My roll number was 2. Yet I remained on the last bench. Complaints and lashes from the cane continued. My palms turned red. I furtively rubbed oil on my painful hands. When I remembered all these things, I thought it was best to forget about school.

For some reason I thought I would go out to the field by myself today. I didn't take the path going by Jhulir Bagan on my way there. I walked through the field in front of Nilu the washerman's house. There was no sign of any village or house from where I was standing now. It was as if this was a tiny field on the bosom of Earth. There were trees shrouded by mist in the distance. I didn't exactly know which village lay in the direction of the horizon. A drongo shrieked *ch-ee-k* and flew off. It rose into the void and did somersaults. Could it see me? I came to a standstill. A sari hanging in Jhulir Bagan flashed before my eyes. My body felt leaden. Was I hearing someone's hoarse voice? I wouldn't advance any further. I hadn't thought that I would come this far. I really liked it if I ever arrived unwittingly at a river, or forest or field. But not for long. I felt like going back. Standing all alone in that yellow vastness, I was the only one I could see there.

Bhombol didn't come with me today. He was terribly unwell. I patted him before I left home. He did not have a fever. I said to him, 'Raise your head!' But he didn't raise it, so I pulled up his snout and examined his gums and teeth. They looked alright. It was nothing in his mouth. Who knows what was wrong with him. He just lay. He hiccupped from time to time. Fleas hovered around him, but he did not move. That's why he stayed back at home. I turned back to look. He was gazing at me with his face buried in his belly.

I had to go past Pireni Ma's hut on my way to the field. The wicker door was shut. Perhaps she had gone to some house for work. My hands went up to my head. If Pireni Ma had said something, I would have replied, 'Just see how long my hair's grown! Could it have become so long in less than a month? My head was shaved a month-and-a-half ago.' Pireni Ma knew that cooking began in my house only after I had foraged the fields. She too went out to the fields. And if she saw me, she would ask, 'Why are you alone?' I would say whatever I had to, but she wasn't there today. After I had gone past her home and the fields, no one knew where I was. Continuing again on the path that I had walked, with the brown-coloured sky over my head, I was walking along the boundary ridge on which bundles of grass had been laid down. Every now and then mustard stalks craned their necks towards the path. I averted them carefully, thinking they would die if I stepped on them. After all, how would they know that this was a walking path? The landowner had strewn the seeds. Those that had slipped out of his hand and fallen beside the ridge had sprouted right there. It was such stalks that lay on the path ahead. I walked mindfully. What was that sound! From high above. Was it an aeroplane? I shaded my eyes and looked. I couldn't see anything. But the sound had indeed come from the sky. There were no clouds, so why couldn't I see anything? I pulled out the sack from under my left arm. My arm had become stiff after having held it in the same position for a long time. I only realised that when I removed the sack. The blurred trees and foliage in the distance became clearer. Just ahead was the road on which bullock carts plied. I would sit on that road and rest for a while. I walked a lot today.

Once I sat on the field, the sun smeared its sweet heat on my body. I had not noticed all these days. But I turned my arms and looked now. There were dark smears of dirt in the crook of my arm. Scars below my knees from the scabies sores that had eaten through the flesh. Although skin had grown there, it hadn't filled the cavity. Perhaps the scars would remain even after I became an adult. There were some scars like that on my face as well. I had been coming down with scabies for some years now. And of all the seasons, it was in winter that this affliction arrived. I scratched and scratched until it bled. And if I smelt my fingers, it wasn't the smell of blood but only that of pus. That was why I was made to sit at the back in school. After all, I was to blame too. It was my body's fault. A body with scabies that smelt of pus. But how could I set it aside?

Perhaps sickness and ailments visited only poor households. I went to the government hospital every now and then. It took about an hour to reach there. Once there, I saw a crowd of bare-bodied folk like us. Mothers would come with their children. Old men with walking sticks. There were very few people with proper clothes on. An open lobby, the shape of the U design on the forehead of Goddess Durga. Doctor Babu sat in the middle of that. The patients sat on the floor. A hand-pulled mat-like fan hung in silence overhead. Doctor Babu called the patients one after the other. When it was my turn, he said, 'Hey boy, come here!'

As I went up to him, he said, 'Haven't I seen you before? What's happened to you now?'

'See here', I said, and bent my head down. I said, 'It itches terribly, Doctor Babu! And pus oozes out.'

'Stand up! Where do you bathe?'

'In the river.'

'Which is your river?'

'Madhumati. No, I mean Nabaganga.'

'Nabaganga? *Eesh*, its water is foul. Foul from all the rotting jute. Terrible!'

I listened in silence. He was right, I didn't know all that. I said quietly, 'But everyone bathes there.'

'Let them, but you shouldn't. Bathe in water from the tubewell or a dug well.'

'There's only one house with a well in our hamlet, but they don't let us touch that. If I wait there with a bucket, they only give me water for drinking. The tubewell is far away, Doctor Babu. And even when I go there, I can only bathe when no one else is there.'

'What on earth are you saying, boy?'

I was silent again.

'What is the bed linen like in your house?'

I stared at him. I couldn't exactly understand him. Doctor Babu wrote on a piece of paper. '*Ki re*, why don't you say anything?'

What could I say, what could I tell him about our plight? If I told him about our tattered kantha, would he understand? No, he wasn't going to ask me any more questions. He had finished writing on the paper. I moved to the queue at the medicine counter.

The compounder was Baba's age. He was very fair-skinned and round-cheeked. Everyone called him 'Rabi-da'. What would I call him?

As soon as he took the prescription from my hand, he blustered, 'So you got scabies!'

'Yes, Babu.'

He scooped out an ointment from a basin using a large, ladle-like spoon. He emptied that on a rectangular sheet made of bamboo leaves. He said, 'Apply it in the morning, in the afternoon, and at night, when you go to bed.'

The fair-skinned Rabi-da was wearing trousers, and I noticed the band around his neck over the loose-fitting white gown that went down to his feet. That gown flashed before my eyes now. Thrice a day. In the morning, afternoon and night. The scabies was gone after I applied the ointment, but it did itch a little after my bath. When I scratched myself, it left a black residue under my nails. It seemed as though my sores were craving affection; once they felt the touch of my nails, the itching ceased.

I hadn't been sitting for long, I remembered all this in just a little while. I remember everything nowadays. Everything. About home, about school. About blowing on singed fingers after removing the lid on the rice pot. I could even see the stick with which dry leaves and suchlike were stuffed into the stove. How the leaves got aflame once they were inside the stove and touched by fire. There was an earthen half-wall beside the stove. Ma used to place the lamp on that. She used a coconut shell to keep salt in. The lamp was no longer lit. The mouth of the lamp was in the same battered state. Baba did not cook at night. I wet muri or chira and had it with sugarcane jaggery. If I was at home, I played next to the kitchen. Play meant making Bhombol sit beside me, while I pretended to be a shopkeeper. I loved playing a shopkeeper. After all, I was going to open a shop when I grew up. While I played, I also thought about what kind of shop it would be.

Setting up shop at the weekly markets with attractive goods. Having a food shop selling boiled eggs and omelettes. Dry sweetmeats. A shop selling sweetmeats like *kathigoja* and *tilekhaja*. I couldn't make up my mind about what I would do. Perhaps Baba would be happy if I opened a shop. He had turned strange somehow. He had to go out to work, and so he did. He didn't speak much after returning home. It had been a long time since he had hit me. He didn't scold me either. I would sell attractive goods that I liked, carrying a large basket on my head, a rolled-up gamchha beneath it. The weekly markets at Alamkhali, Ichhekhada and Haurer Haat. Of course, the one at Magura too. It was close by. If only Ma had been alive to see me as a shopkeeper.

The market contractor in our weekly market charged a rent of an anna. Was the rent high here, or was it low? I thought about all that too. An idea came to me—what if I set up a shop selling salt! After all, it was needed in every household. I would buy a sackful and keep it at home after packing it in a taro leaf, and winding a string around it four times. Just as my cousin, Badal-da, sold salt at the weekly market. After measuring out the salt, he would place it on a taro leaf, fold that four times, and then wind and knot a string around it, before giving the string a sudden tug to tear it loose.

I would collect the taro leaves myself. There was a forest of taro in the place known as the fairies' pit. Taro leaf was round and beautiful to look at. A real shop after all the make-believe ones! I would pay obeisance to Ma before leaving for the shop. There would be a picture of Ma. Asleep, with her eyes shut.

Couldn't there be a photo like that? With all of us around her. Who else would be there in the picture? I don't know. Let the time come, I would take care of it. Chhor-da had told me that Nabakumar was opening a photo studio very soon.

Even if there wasn't a picture of Ma alive, the picture of her asleep with her eyes shut would suffice. Putting down the basket of salt, I would offer pranam to Ma with my eyes closed. And then placing the basket on my head, I would leave for the market. Everything would get sold with Ma's blessings. Coins would jingle in my purse. If I received notes, I would keep those in the other pocket. The purse should never be empty. There should always be at least a coin in it. There were several other rules too. I would find out about those. If the business was successful, I wouldn't let Baba go out to work any more. He would stay at home. He would make a barrier around the house with creepers or date palm leaves. There was no fence, but if plants and bushes were tied together, that would make a fence. Cows kept coming in now since there was no barrier. We could plant some vegetables and greens using spade and hoe. There was no need to sell those, it was fine if it met our own needs.

I had so many dreams. So far I had only been dreaming of the things that came to my mind. I had no clue where I was. I had no idea that I had arrived at the gardens on one side of the field. So many things came to my mind. Things I liked; things I didn't like. Amidst all that, I lost all track of when I got up from my sitting place. Here were all the tall trees, wooded clumps and gardens. I turned around to look at the field. How small the babla tree with the drongo looked. And how blurred the yellow field appeared from here. The mustard stalks craning their necks towards the path floated before my eyes. Did the peasants on the fields or others who walked along the path tread carefully like me? If they didn't, and they stepped on the stalks, they wouldn't survive.

Heck! Why should one worry about such trivial things? But I saw them as our crop-beings. If I came across something very small and unloved, I would never forget that. It would grow into a plant. There would be grains of crop on every stalk, and then they would dry up. The landowner would cut them at the base and take them away. But would anyone remember their colourful flowers when they were in their infancy? Their growth, their basking in the sunlight, their swaying in the breeze. How much they did in a short span of time. A field decorated in yellow. And then one day …

I didn't know whether or not such thoughts were correct. I mentioned them because they came to mind. I didn't really have anyone whom I could tell them to. Could one trample and kill the tender stalks that seemed to want to advance with their trunks raised? If I said this to Ashit or Dipu, they would laugh. I didn't have any other friends in the hamlet. I remembered someone, our teacher from Class III. What if I asked him, 'Sir, should anyone trample the necks of the newly sprouted stalks? I had gone to the field. I was looking out for them.' Like me, he too would have said, 'You were right, you did well. Your thinking is correct.'

For some reason, I didn't feel like entering Jhulir Bagan today. The path with jungle on both sides converged with the road going from the Shibrampur Union Board to Magura. This road along the Nabaganga went past the banyan tree near our house and reached the riverbank, at the Tibet company's jetty. I now realised that the route I had taken was not so far away from the Kalikatala crematorium.

I had never been there. I imagined the place, with torn mats strewn in the nearby jungle and discarded, half-burnt logs of wood. Earthen pitchers. Were people there, like they were at the Shatdowa crematorium? Tiny huts. A man with matted locks. *Bolo Hari, Hari Bol!* Why was I thinking about all this? After all, I didn't want to. But still. Such nonsense floated up all of a sudden. If I were strong, what all I would have done! If only we were rich folk. If only I had a knife—I felt very angry nowadays—I would have roamed around with that. Everyone would see it. The knife in my hand. I would stand with it when it was play time in the hamlet, and say, 'So tell me, will you include me now!'

All kinds of rubbish. It was rubbish after all. I laughed. I walked on one side of the road on which bullock carts plied. Thanks to the muddy slime, it was as if a long, high mound separated the jungle on the two sides. With the plying of the carts during the rainy season, the muddy slime was pushed to the middle. After the rains, it dried up and remained there like a small wall. I was walking along one side now. If I went home empty-handed, that would be the first time. I hadn't even undone the knot on the sack. Hey, there's a mongoose! I jumped and frightened it. It ran and darted for cover in the assheora jungle. I was almost home. I could spot the roof of our hut through the gap between the banana leaves.

The period of impurity was long over. But I still wasn't going to school. It had been a long time, and I didn't feel like going any more. Many of the boys in my class had stopped attending. They had discontinued their studies. They had either joined their fathers in the fields, or set up shop. I encountered them when I went to the weekly market, or on the road. If one ran into them during school time, they turned their heads away in shame. One day I spotted Wahab sitting with pumpkins in the vegetable market. He was the one who called out to me. 'Hey Ratan!'

'Why aren't you in school?'

'Abba died. Ma said, how can you continue your studies? Set up shop in the market. So I've come with vegetables.'

I gazed at him. He was wearing a vest that was torn at the shoulder. There were a few pumpkins in the basket. Some cucumbers. Did he feel ashamed that I was looking at him? Was that why he said, 'Take a cucumber.'

'What's the price?'

'*Dhur*! It's grown at home. How can I take money from a classmate.'

'*Na re*. I'll take it if you take one paisa.'

'Then you needn't take it.' And then he asked, 'Does the Class III Sir ask about me?'

Many boys liked Sir, just like I did. 'I don't know, I haven't been to school for a long time.'

'Why is that? Why didn't you go to school?'

'My Ma too ...' And as soon as I said that, my eyes brimmed with tears. I made to leave, without waiting for his reply. But he stood up at once and held me back. He put a cucumber into my bag. 'You have to take this.'

If I had stayed on, I could have asked him, 'How much profit do you make, Wahab? Which weekly markets do you go to? How much is the market contractor's rent?' But everything got muddled up. I hadn't realised anything seeing him. Muslim folk did not shave their heads when their parents died. I only found out because he told me. So many boys lost their Ma or Baba at an early age, I suppose they set up shop like this after that. Perhaps I too was going to join their squad.

I thought about it. I was plagued by a flurry of thoughts. Perhaps it was inarguable. How would one feed and clothe oneself if one continued going to school? But if one set up shop, one handled money. One could buy things for home if one wanted to. A tonic for Baba to get well. A shawl. Baba wore a fotua. Once I opened my shop, I would buy a shirt for him. And then I would surprise him with it, and say, 'Try it on, Baba, if it's small, I'll exchange it.'

Even before I reached the road going to Shibrampur, I noticed that mud had been piled up on the road. Earth was being excavated from the adjacent low-lying land. The spade hardly had to be swung. One struck the soil with a flick of the wrist and lifted a clod to the basket. The earth-cutters climbed up to the road with their baskets. They stood in a row, like a line of ants. The baskets had sticks attached to them. The sticks helped transfer the baskets from one head to another. The earth travelled for a short distance. And then it was dumped. Bits of clay fell on the eyelids of the men with the baskets, concealing them. So that even those who knew them wouldn't recognise them now.

The road was being raised. People were clearing the adjacent jungle and advancing. One could get back on the road after proceeding for a short distance by the side. I too stepped down and walked beside the bamboo palms on the side, moving the shyaora plants on the way. Suddenly a thick lath struck my chest. I screamed, 'Oof!' A man turned his head around and said, 'Hey, did you get hurt? I didn't realise ...' And at once he rushed towards me and patted my chest. 'Where did you get hurt? Let me see if you got a cut.'

I pressed my chest, and said, 'No, there's no cut, Chacha.'

'You poor boy! I've given you a bruise.'

'Oh it's nothing, I get so many bruises,' I said, making light of the matter.

'Where had you gone?'

'To forage for cow dung and fuelwood.'

'But there's paddy on the fields. Didn't you get any twigs?'

'No. I didn't feel like it, so I'm going back home.'

'Where's your house?'

'Near the banyan tree.'

'Oh, then you're almost there. Come, let's walk together.'

I walked ahead, rubbing my hand on my chest. Our road was being built, and so this injury didn't seem painful at all. They had begun laying the road from this place. Perhaps after this it would go along our banyan tree, the marketplace, and the Kali temple before it reached the town. There was a metalled road thereafter. No, I didn't go anywhere. Not even to forage for twigs in the garden of the crematorium at Kalikatala. This was the first time I had set out with a sack and then returned empty-handed.

Bhombol Is Very Sick

Would Bhombol die very soon?

Earlier, if crows came to the courtyard, he would bark at them. Even after the birds flapped their wings and flew off hurriedly to a branch of the guava tree, he stood under the tree, and what a ruckus he made! He made me tremble. As if he was saying, 'Be off with you, or else I'll leap just now!'

But there was none of all that now. He just looked at them as he lay on the ground. The birds blithely strutted around, pecking at insects and suchlike. Bhombol observed everything. But he couldn't even raise his head. His eyes were rheumy. Flies sat on the rheum. A whole row of them. Bhombol then shut his eyes. What on earth had happened to him?

I had to bring his food to him and call him. He rose somehow. Poor thing! His belly was hollow. One could count his protruding ribs. Why were ailments visiting our household time and again? This wasn't a minor fever or something, it was a major ailment like Ma's. Earlier, after he was served rice, he used to gulp it down. But now he gazed at me with a strange look in his eye. 'Why are you looking at me like that, Bhombol?'

I patted his back. 'Eat. Eat slowly … what's happened to you?'

He understood everything I said. He loved the pap with leftovers of fish, but on most days, khichuri was prepared. Dal and rice. With a mash of greens. He wouldn't eat that, so I gave him some rice with a watery dal. With a little bit of salt. He ate that, although I think he had lost the sense of taste. If he was given a curry made with small fish, he could eat a bit of that as well. It was only on the days of the weekly market that purchases were made. Baba brought home some fish. There had been no fish for some months now. That still continued. Taro, potatoes and spinach is what we ate. I ran my hand over Bhombol's tail. He wagged it. I sat with him until he finished his food. I didn't leave like I used to earlier. After all, he was all I had. What if something happened to him.

I had heard that there was a veterinary hospital at Bhaynar Mor. Where exactly was it? Which building? Had I seen it? Was it near the cattle-pound? Wouldn't someone show me where it was if I asked them? They would surely do that when they saw me carrying Bhombol in my arms, and I told them about his ailment. But how would I take him? After all, he was no longer a puppy. I had to take him somehow or the other. I would go by myself. He would walk as much as he could. I would carry him after that, and then put him down after a while to rest. I would tell him, 'Walk a bit now! Can you do that?' But given his condition, would I be able to lift him up?

I brought a rag and sat down in front of him. He gave off a really foul smell. Let it be. After all, even Ma gave off a smell towards the end. But did I stop going to her because of that? And Bhombol had been in our house ever since he was a tiny puppy. I called out to him, 'Come!'

He lifted up his head and looked at me. He looked suspiciously at the rag in my hand. 'Show me your face, let me wipe away the rheum. I have to take you to the hospital, don't I! What if Doctor Babu scolds me for not wiping your eyes? Get up now!'

I realised he was worried seeing the tattered rag. I patted him affectionately. I had never approached him with such a rag. Seeing the unknown thing, he looked alarmed. I said to him, 'Hey, it's just a piece of cloth from the house, there's nothing to be afraid of.' But he didn't believe me. He whimpered. As if to say, 'What's this, Dada?'

As soon as I held his neck and made to wipe his eyes, he moved his head away with a jerk and stood up.

'Come now, don't be scared, it's nothing, I just want to wipe your eyes. Would you like it if Doctor Babu called you a filthy dog? Come here.'

He wanted to free himself from my grip. He didn't seem to believe me. He kept eyeing the rag dangling from my hand and moving away. No matter how much I told him, 'Come, there's nothing to be scared of', he only stretched himself lazily.

Why was he doing that? After all, he trusted me! He enjoyed it if I pulled his ear, or lifted his leg up in the air. He nuzzled my chest, as if to ask me for more. That was how we played. When I went for my bath, I only had to get my gamchha and call him. And then we ran, stopping only when we reached the riverbank. No, it wasn't enough just to reach there. We got into the water after everyone there finished bathing. Bhombol sat on his haunches at the riverbank. We waited in silence. Bhombol knew that his Dada liked to bathe all alone. And not just bathe. I would call out to him and then plunge into the water, and emerge at the other bank. I would raise my hand and call out, 'Bho-m-bol!'

He would get off his haunches. He readied himself, as if he was about to chase birds. He was restless. As if he would jump into the water at once! But what was Bhombol thinking of today? It suddenly occurred to me if it was alright to wipe his eyes. After all, one didn't adorn a sick person. His rheumy eyes were part of his ailment. What if by doing that, it spread to the rest of his body? No, perhaps he didn't want me to do that. Perhaps it wasn't right. It was as if Bhombol was saying, 'Let Doctor Babu look at me first, you can do it after that!'

Let Bhombol be as he is. Should I inform Ashit? Should I tell him, 'You're the one who gave Bhombol to me when he was small, he's unwell today, I need to take him to the hospital, will you come with me?'

I couldn't remember where I heard about the veterinary hospital. And then I suddenly remembered. A man was once walking to the town carrying a goat in his arms. The goat's head was drooping despite that. He was headed for the hospital. Down the road going to the town, and then straight to Bhaynar Mor along the road going past the college. I remembered that was where the hospital was. When I went to Ashit in the morning, he was silent and mouthed 'Baba' and shook his head. I knew his parents forbid him from hanging around with me. He was cautioning me since his Baba was at home. But, after all, I hadn't come to do anything wrong. Speaking quite loudly now, I said, 'Our Bhombol is very sick, he needs to be taken to the hospital, will you come with me, Ashit? I won't be able to manage on my own, you could help me if necessary. He'll survive if we take him to the hospital! Come along!'

What was wrong with that? Bhombol was a helpless creature, and it was only for him that I had come. It was because of him that I was breaking the rules. Ashit's signal meant, go from here! But I didn't. I don't know how I mustered up courage. That's why I spoke out loud.

Ashit stared at me blankly. As he communicated with me, he reached the entrance of the house. Where his Baba might be. 'Are you taking him to the hospital?'

The moment he said that, Kaka emerged and said, 'What's happened, boy? Who's sick?'

'Our Bhombol is very sick, Kaka! He's just been lying down for the last few days. I want to take him to the hospital. Can Ashit come along?'

'That's fine! Take him. It's a good thing.'

I used to think that everyone thought we were bad folk. But I saw for myself today that it was not so. A social boycott had been imposed on our family. I was unhappy about that, but now I felt cheered up. I said, 'Put on your shirt and pants, Ashit!'

There was no impediment now. Ashit's family was poor too, but they did not belong to a low caste like ours. Like with the other houses in the village, I could not enter their house as and when I pleased. Ashit couldn't call me to play with him even if he wanted to. But for some reason, it was me that he called on the days he went foraging in the fields. We talked a lot as we made our way to the fields and gardens. Like friends did. Ashit had discontinued his studies last term. He now sat with Kaka in their rice shop. He was learning shopkeeping early. Ashit put on his shirt and pants while I waited in their courtyard.

Three of my friends had left school. Two of them in Class II, and Ashit in Class III. In truth, there were so many households in the village! But I didn't know of anyone from any household who had a job. A job meant education. And I couldn't think of anyone who had passed the Matric examination. Shanti-di married Subodh from Bunopara, near the town, and changed her religion. She had come after her marriage to pay her respects to her father, Sudhir Kaka. The rickshaw was standing at the roadside. She offered pranam to Kaka, who was sitting in the veranda, and left at once. I heard that the same Shanti-di got a job in the hospital. Had Didi passed her Matric? All those who lived in the village now had shops in the market. Ashit and Wahab had learnt the trade. But when would I? Was it too late already? And hadn't Baba said that he would sell the house? If he did that, which village would we go to then? Where would Baba take us after he sold the house? Could one start a shop there?

Ashit set out with me. We ran almost all the way to my house. It was Ashit who carried Bhombol in his arms. He lifted him up and said, 'Hey, do you recognise me?'

But Bhombol seemed not to hear anything. He looked on indifferently, the way he did when crows and other birds alighted on the courtyard. When Ashit went to lift him up, I thought he would resist. But no, he blithely went along. I said, 'Did you see? How sick he must be to go to a stranger!'

Ashit protested, 'Why stranger? Hasn't he seen me before? He knows my face! Dogs never forget a person once they've seen him. And we live in the same hamlet, don't we!'

Ashit was right. It was I who had imagined otherwise.

Before we left the house, Ashit said, 'Latch the door.'

'Latch?' I laughed, and said, 'Rubbish! Nothing will happen, what's there at home! And besides, do thieves come in broad daylight? Anyway, since you're telling me ...' I went and latched the door.

Ashit set off, carrying Bhombol. We had to go past the persimmon tree. The same path then fringed the lake, and then went through Jolapara till we reached Bhaynar Mor. I ran and caught up with Ashit. Bhombol rested his head on Ashit's shoulder and gazed at the row of trees on the way. The poor thing was utterly helpless.

Some Truths and Some Lies

The room on the western side had been locked up for a long time. Ever since my dadas left. I climbed up the guava tree and observed the small plants that had sprouted in various places on the roof. With white blotches around them. The sun was terribly hot now. Was that why a thin wisp of smoke rose from the roof? I thought so. The shon-grass thatch had rotted. The thatch was still sodden inside from the rains. That had got heated up in the sun, and this smoke was the steam rising up from within. The thatch had also given way in some places. That meant the condition of the bamboo trusses beneath it wasn't sound either. They had rotted too. Or else the roof wouldn't have given way like that. I climbed a bit higher and spotted some kind of vine that had come up a wall. I would probably see more damage if I climbed any higher. Perhaps after some time the whole house would be a jungle full of plants and vines. Baba used to take care of such things earlier. Did it mean that we would really leave this house and go away elsewhere? Is that why he wasn't spending any money on repairing the house?

Repairs would require a lot of money. But there was no money. Even I knew that. We would have eaten well if there had been money. It's because there was no money that we faced such a lot of hardship. The shon-grass-thatch had to be bought, and bamboo poles too. The entire old roof had to be discarded and a new one had to be laid. So it was best to leave things as they were. Why waste money unnecessarily. I couldn't figure out anything. I slowly made my way down. If I stayed any longer, I would feel dejected.

I went up to the threshing space in the desolate house. I wanted to see all the places in the house. Since no one was taking care of the house, I would do that. After all, the house belonged to me too. I had such fond memories of this house, but who would I say that to? I was born in this courtyard. This soil was my mother. If I weren't so young, I would have worked hard myself and kept the house in order. The walls of the house had not been plastered with cow dung in a long time. There was salt deposition on the walls and it was crumbly. Although the walls were still standing, the salted mud was simply raining down. If the walls and floors were not plastered with cow dung, there was bound to be salt deposition. The earthen walls were simply crumbling away because they had not been taken care of.

There were no walls around the threshing space. There were posts going up from the ground, which defined the space. There was a lath fence all around. That too was all askew now. Almost all the laths had termite trails of dry mud on them. Some of them had been completely hollowed out by termites. The place had a very melancholic look as it continued to stand under the sun, rain and mist. I never paid any attention to this space because I never went there. But it was a part of the house after all. The props of the wooden threshing implement were covered in dust and grime. Leaves had blown in and then remained there. The props were almost buried under the leaves. I wanted to see the wood underneath. Ma used to flatten rice to the rhythm of the thresher. The *dhakush-kush* sound. My eyes were brimming again. No, I wouldn't think about all that. My lips were pouted, ready to sob. I was a grown up now, but the habit of crying seemed not to have left me.

I examined everything closely today. It was our household that was the poorest one in the village. Others had tin-sheet roofs. And even if they had a shon-grass-thatched roof, it was well maintained. There would be a floral design on the wall, made with empty cigarette packets. A boat drawn on the low wall of the veranda. A fish. But our walls had not been plastered with cow dung in a long time. I wished the house was nice, and that I too could draw something. If nothing else, I would draw Bhombol looking at the sky and howling. I got down from the threshing space and moved towards the kitchen. But no, I stopped. If I went in there I would only see the things touched by Ma's hands. I didn't want to feel dejected again.

It was only Baba, Chhor-da and me at home now. If anyone asked about my two elder brothers, Baba made something up. He said they had got a job in a textile mill in Daulatpur. Sometimes he said they were working in a big shop in Dhaka, or that they were in Jessore. He said he would send me there too. The truth was that my dadas had gone to Calcutta. Was that where I would go too? Would I have to leave? I remembered Ma's father's house in Ramdevganti. A cloth bundle tucked under my arm. Me holding Ma's finger. Walking the long way to Ramdevganti. The tamarind tree. With the primary school beside it. Ma had studied till Class II there. The tin-sheet roof of the school was visible. On the way, Ma would point towards the marketplaces of the villages Satyajitpur and Binodpur. And I remembered going to school in Magura, crossing the swaying bamboo bridge. Would I have to leave all this behind?

Calcutta was apparently a very big city. Much bigger than Dhaka. Bigger than America even? I had heard in school that America was the wealthiest country on earth. It had buildings that touched the sky. The twinkling tail lights of aeroplanes were visible from those tall buildings. As were the heads of the people sitting by the windows. If I went to Calcutta, I would see for myself whether it was smaller than America. Baba had told us, 'You mustn't tell anyone. You'll go to school there.'

No, I hadn't told anyone. But I had just got promoted to Class IV. New books. What would happen to them? Why had Baba bought them if he was going to send me to Calcutta? I went to school. Like I did earlier. No one viewed me as poorly as before now. But my place was still on the last bench. Let that be, if what Baba said was true, I wouldn't be here for much longer. Did that mean I wouldn't get admitted to Model High School, or to Magura Academy after my next promotion? But I was really keen to enter high school. Then I would appear for the Matric exam after just a few years there. And after passing the Matric, there was IA. That meant going to Magura College. Had Baba spoken about selling the house because we were going away to Calcutta? He and Chhor-da didn't talk about such things in front of me. I don't know why they turned silent if I happened to be there. Was it so that I wouldn't tell anyone? But why would I do that? Did anyone blabber about their secret household matters?

Whenever such thoughts crossed my mind I felt the urge to study. But the poverty! When I ate chira or muri instead of rice, I thought I ought to discontinue school like Wahab and Ashit, and open a shop. If I did that, Baba's difficulties would lessen. Chhor-da and I would be able to run the household somehow or the other. I had not gone to school for a long time because I had kind of decided that. After all, almost three or four months had passed since Ma's death.

Did Ma's brother in Ramdevganti know? Had Baba ever told Ma that we would leave this house and go away one day? What if Ma had then said that she would not leave this house and go anywhere. I needed to think about that. I would want to know from Baba how Ma had responded. But when would I ask him that? I always felt scared to talk to Baba. And now it wasn't so much my fright—Baba himself had turned very silent. He had to go to work, and so he went. Didn't my dadas send any money? Perhaps there wouldn't be so much hardship if they did. Chhor-da hadn't been able to do anything of his own. I would have known if he had. I don't know how much of a manual trade he had picked up. Perhaps not enough to start earning something. Should I tell Baba, 'I won't study any more Baba! I don't like it. Let me set up a small shop.' All he had to say was 'yes'. That would decide matters. But he had spoken to me about studying. About getting into a school in Calcutta. Then why did Baba buy the new books?

I couldn't figure out what I should do. If I found out that Ma was not in favour of selling the house, there was no way I would go. If I observed any arrangements to send me off, I would run away at dawn before that. Yes, I would catch a bus from Bhayna Mor. Straight to Jessore. I would ask people how to get to Daulatpur. I would ask which bus went to Dhaka. Since Ma didn't want it, I would not leave the country. This soil. Let everyone leave. Ma and I would stay behind. Ma's body was here. The fact that I stayed behind would always be in my mind, and I would be able to tell her, your little son

Ratan too stayed back like you. But how would I tell Baba that! That's all I thought about. Nothing else. I only needed to know what Ma had said. I couldn't stop thinking about that.

They had to listen to me because I was much older now. If I stayed back, I would have to be alone. I would have to work. I didn't know what work I would do, but if I went to a snack shop in the big city and said I wanted to work there, wouldn't the shopkeeper take me? I would say, 'I can do everything. I can wash utensils. Clean the floor. Everything. Just give me a bit to eat. I'll sleep in the shop itself at night.' Wouldn't he take me? I think he would. Once he saw my skinny body and my shaven head with a little bit of hair, he would know. What if he asked me, who do you have at home? I would tell him some truths and some lies. My Ma died. My Baba and Dada left me behind and went away to Calcutta. That's why I am looking for work. The shopkeeper would surely pity me. He would take me on. 'Alright! Get to work!'

I had been thinking for the last few days about what all I would need if I lived by myself. And as I did that, I looked for Ma's belongings. What would I take? There were a couple of saris. One of them was torn. She stopped wearing saris once she fell ill. She only had a chemise on. No, not the chemise. I took down the torn sari from the bamboo shelf. Next to the earthen pot with rice was another empty pot. I put the sari inside and laid the pot upside down. The good shirt I wore to school, and another one to wear at other times. That was always hanging in the room. That's all I would take. Oh yes, there was also a shawl. A blue shawl with leaf designs. I would take that too. I would wrap that around myself in winter, and use it as a blanket as well. There was nothing else to take. After all, I wasn't going to study anymore.

Doctor Babu had given Bhombol an injection. I didn't think he would be quiet when he did. I had shut my eyes. It was Ashit who did whatever was needed. Bhombol was in his arms all the while. He was much better then. How sick he had been! I was scared he wouldn't survive. Anyway, he was m-u-c-h better later. But he didn't pounce on the crows like he did earlier. Perhaps he thought, let them be. After all, they lived in the same village too. They, he and Ratan Dada. Let's all be together. Perhaps if he didn't see them now he would wonder why they hadn't come.

I was worried about Bhombol. If I went away, where would he live? The other day, I lifted up his neck and scratched him there, and I asked him, 'Hey, what will you do if you discover that I'm no longer there?'

He seemed not to hear anything. His eyes were shut as he relished the scratching. And the affection. Or was he thinking, there's no way you can leave this house.

No dear, I'll surely leave, just you see.

Tears ran down my face. They fell on Bhombol. I held him tight.

Also from ekadā

Also from ekadā

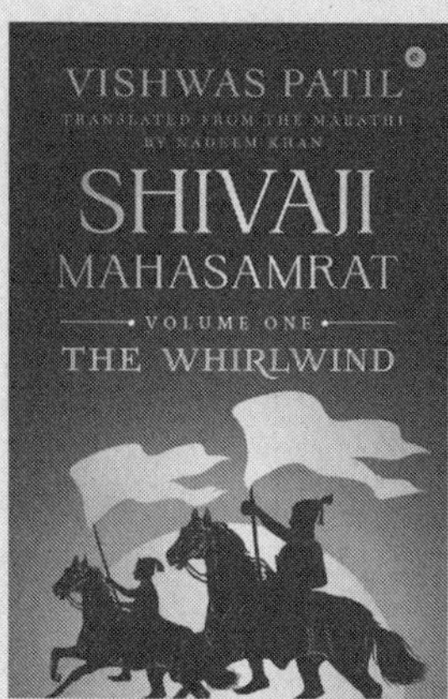

Also from ekadā

Also from ekadā

Also from ekadā

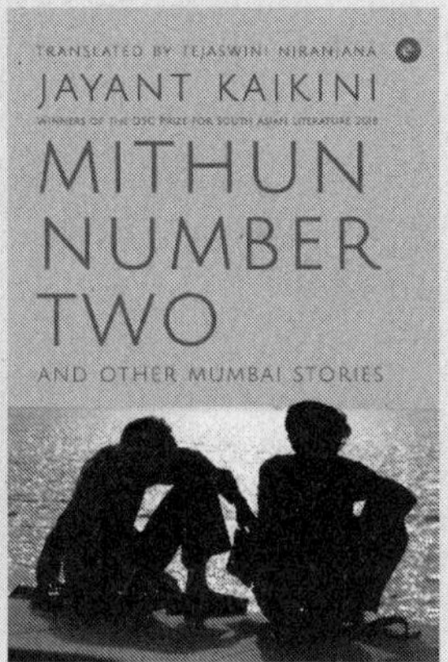

Also from ekadā

Also from ekadā

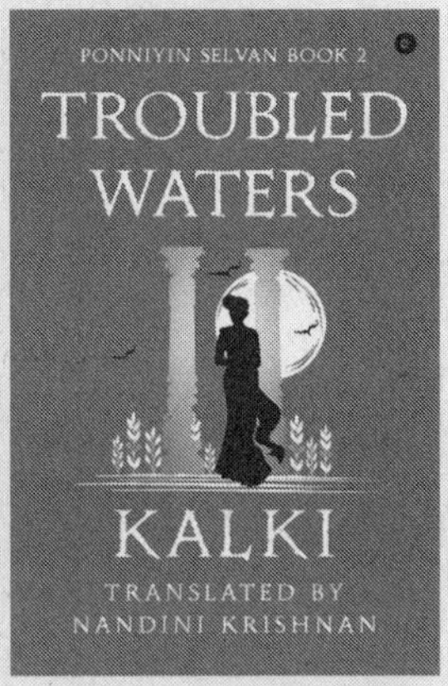

Also from ekadā